Playing w[...]
Pres[...]
Aescl[...]

# THE ORESTEIA
## A Trilogy of Greek Tragedies
## FOR KIDS
(The melodramatic version!)

Based off Aeschylus' orignal play
translated by E.D.A. Morshead

For 5-25 actors, or kids of all ages who want to have fun!
Creatively modified by Amanda Ruby & Brendan P. Kelso
Cover stage illustrated by Shana Hallmeyer
Cover illustrations by Ron Leishman

3 Melodramatic Modifications
for 3 different group sizes:

5-11 actors

10-19 actors

15-25 actors

PlayingWithPlays.com

# Table Of Contents

Foreword ................................................................... Pg 4
School, Afterschool, and Summer classes ............ Pg 6
Performance Rights ................................................ Pg 7
5-11 Actors ............................................................... Pg 8
10-19 Actors ............................................................ Pg 28
15-25 Actors ............................................................ Pg 50
Pronunciations ........................................................ Pg 74
Special Thanks ........................................................ Pg 75
Sneak Peeks at other Playing With Plays ............. Pg 76
About the Authors .................................................. Pg 100

To the theatre teachers of
Houston ISD who inspire children for greatness.
**EVERY. SINGLE. DAY.**
-BPK

To my husband who makes me better in every way and my kids whose talent, humor, and smarts make me proud to be their mom.
-AR

---

Playing with Plays™ – Aeschylus' The Oresteia for Kids

Copyright © 2004-2023 by Brendan P. Kelso. All rights reserved. Used with permission by Playing with Plays LLC
Some characters on the cover are © Ron Leishman ToonClipart.com. Used with permission.

No part of this book may be reproduced in any form or by any electronic or mechanical means, including photocopying, recording, information storage or retrieval systems now known or to be invented, without permission in writing from the publisher, except by a reviewer, who may quote brief passages in a review, written for inclusion within a periodical. Any members of education institutions wishing to photocopy part or all of the work for classroom use, or publishers who would like to obtain permission to include the work in an anthology, should send their inquiries to the publisher. We monitor the internet for cases of piracy and copyright infringement/violations. We will pursue all cases within the full extent of the law.

CAUTION: Professionals and amateurs are hereby warned that all plays published by Playing With Plays may be produced only pursuant to a signed written license and are subject to payment of a royalty. The plays are fully protected under the copyright laws of the United States, Canada, the United Kingdom, and all other countries of the Berne Union,. All rights, including dramatic (both amateur and professional), motion picture, radio, television, recitation, public reading, internet, and any method of photographic reproduction are strictly reserved.

Whenever a Playing With Plays play is performed, the following must be included on all programs, printing and advertising for the play: © 2004-2023 by Brendan P. Kelso. All rights reserved. Performed under license from, Playing with Plays LLC, www.PlayingWithPlays.com.

## For performance rights please see page 6 of this book or contact:

## contact@PlayingWithPlays.com

-Please note, for certain circumstances, we do waive copyright and performance fees.
Rules subject to change

www.PlayingWithPlays.com

Printed in the United States of America
Published by Playing With Plays LLC

ISBN: 9781954571105

# Foreword

When I was in high school there was something about Shakespeare that appealed to me. Not that I understood it mind you, but there were clear scenes and images that always stood out in my mind. Romeo & Juliet, "Romeo, Romeo; wherefore art thou Romeo?"; Julius Caesar, "Et tu Brute"; Macbeth, "Double, Double, toil and trouble"; Hamlet, "to be or not to be"; A Midsummer Night's Dream, all I remember about this was a wickedly cool fairy and something about a guy turning into a donkey that I thought was pretty funny. It was not until I started analyzing Shakespeare's plays as an actor that I realized one very important thing, I still didn't understand them. Seriously though, it's tough enough for adults, let alone kids. Then it hit me, why don't I make a version that kids could perform, but make it easy for them to understand with a splash of Shakespeare lingo mixed in? And voila! A melodramatic masterpiece was created! They are intended to be melodramatically fun!

**THE PLAYS:** There are 3 plays within this book, for three different group sizes. The reason: to allow educators or parents to get the story across to their children regardless of the size of their group. As you read through the plays, there are several lines that are highlighted. These are actual lines from the original book. I am a little more particular about the kids saying these lines verbatim. But the rest, well... have fun!

The entire purpose of this book is to instill the love of a classic story, as well as drama, into the kids.

And when you have children who have a passion for something, they will start to teach themselves, with or without school.

These plays are intended for pure fun. Please DO NOT have the kids learn these lines verbatim, that would be a complete waste of creativity. But do have them basically know their lines and improvise wherever they want as long as it pertains to telling the story. Because that is the goal of an actor: to tell the story. In A Midsummer Night's Dream, I once had a student playing Quince question me about one of her lines, "but in the actual story, didn't the Mechanicals state that 'they would hang us'?" I thought for a second and realized that she had read the story with her mom, and she was right. So I let her add the line she wanted and it added that much more fun, it made the play theirs. I have had kids throw water on the audience, run around the audience, sit in the audience, lose their pumpkin pants (size 30 around a size 15 doesn't work very well, but makes for some great humor!) and most importantly, die all over the stage. The kids love it.

One last note: if you want some educational resources, loved our plays, want to tell the world how much your kids loved performing Shakespeare, want to insult someone with our Shakespeare Insult Generator, or are just a fan of Shakespeare, then hop on our website and have fun:

### PlayingWithPlays.com

With these notes, I'll see you on the stage, have fun, and break a leg!

## SCHOOL, AFTERSCHOOL, and SUMMER CLASSES

I've been teaching these plays as afterschool and summer programs for quite some time. Many people have asked what the program is, therefore, I have put together a basic formula so any teacher or parent can follow and have melodramatic success! As well, many teachers use my books in a variety of ways. You can view the formula and many more resources on my website at: PlayingWithPlays.com

- Brendan

## OTHER PLAYS AND FULL LENGTH SCRIPTS

We have over 30 different titles, as well as a full-length play in 4-acts for theatre groups: Shakespeare's Hilarious Tragedies. You can see all of our other titles on our website here: PlayingWithPlays.com/books

As well, you can see a sneak peek at some of those titles at the back of this book.

And, if you ever have any questions, please don't hesitate to ask at: Contact@PlayingWithPlays.com

# LICENSES AND ROYALTIES

All performances and other productions require the issuance of a license. Here are the basic guidelines:

1) Please contact us! We always LOVE to hear about a school or group performing our books! We would also love to share photos and brag about your program as well! (with your permission, of course)

2) We require that you purchase a copy of the play for the director/teacher and each kid in the show.

3) If you are a group and DO NOT charge your kids to be in the production, contact us about our educational rates to get a copy in each kid's hands inexpensively. (we will make this work for you!)

4) If you are a group and DO charge your kids to be in the production, (i.e. afterschool program, summer camp), contact us for bulk (10 books or more) or educator's discounts.

5) If you are a group and DO NOT charge the audience to see the plays, please see our website FAQs (www.PlayingWithPlays.com) to see if you are eligible to waive the performance license(s) (most performances are eligible)

6) If you are a group and DO charge the audience to see the performance, please see our website FAQs for performance licensing fees (this includes performances for donations and competitions)

Any other questions or comments, please see our website or email us at:

contact@PlayingWithPlays.com

# The 15-Minute or so THE ORESTEIA for Kids

by Aeschylus
Creatively modified by
Amanda Ruby & Brendan P. Kelso
## 5-11 Actors

### CAST OF CHARACTERS:

[1]**CHORUS 1:** Elder of Argos
[1]**CHORUS 2:** Servant
[1]**CHORUS 3:** Fury
[2]**CLYTEMNESTRA:** Wife of Agamemnon
[3]**AGAMEMNON:** King of Argos for a short period
[4]**CASSANDRA:** Princess of Troy
[5]**AEGISTHUS:** Clytemnestra's secret boyfriend, Agamemnon's cousin
[5]**ORESTES:** Son of Clytemnestra and Agamemnon
[4]**ELECTRA:** Daughter of Clytemnestra and Agamemnon
[3]**APOLLO:** self-absorbed God of the Sun, Music, and other cool things
[2]**ATHENA:** Goddess of Wisdom

Characters with no lines:
Soldiers/Guards/Servants/Jurors

[1]Same actor can play CHORUS 1, 2, and 3
[2]Same actor can play CLYTEMNESTRA and ATHENA
[3]Same actor can play AGAMEMNON and APOLLO
[4]Same actor can play CASSANDRA and ELECTRA
[5]Same actor can play AEGISTHUS and ORESTES

*anyone not on stage can play extra Soldiers/Guards/Servants/Jurors

## ACT 1 - Agamemnon

*(Someone walks by with a sign that says, "PLAY 1 - AGAMEMNON - KINGDOM OF ARGOS"; CHORUS 1 enters)*

**CHORUS 1:** *(to audience)* I hope we hear news of the war soon. Ten livelong years have rolled away since the Trojan War began. As an elder, I know all the stories. Long ago, King Atreus was murdered by his brother. Then his sons, Agamemnon and Menelaus, fled to Sparta.

*(enter AGAMEMNON)*

**AGAMEMNON:** My brother and I have to flee or we're next!

*(AGAMEMNON exits screaming)*

**CHORUS 1:** The King of Sparta let Agamemnon marry his daughter, Clytemnestra.

*(enter AGAMEMNON and CLYTEMNESTRA)*

**AGAMEMNON:** I do!

**CLYTEMNESTRA:** I do, too!

*(AGAMEMNON and CLYTEMNESTRA exit)*

**CHORUS 1:** Awwwwe. *(sniffling)* I always cry at weddings. *(blows nose)* His brother, Menelaus became King of Sparta and married the most beautiful woman in the world, Helen. Then, Agamemnon returned from Sparta.

*(AGAMEMNON enters)*

**AGAMEMNON:** I need to kill my uncle and reclaim the throne!

**CHORUS 1:** Oh, just like Hamlet, no wait, Lion King!

**AGAMEMNON:** NO! Those stories were based on this story!

**CHORUS 1:** Seriously? Cool!

**AGAMEMNON:** Yes, cool. Now, do you mind? I'm a bit busy here, taking back my kingdom and all.

**CHORUS 1:** Oh, yeah, sorry. *(AGAMEMNON runs offstage)* And then, a few years later, King Paris of Troy stopped in for a not-so-friendly visit. He stole Helen!

*(scream from backstage; enter AGAMEMNON)*

**AGAMEMNON:** I'm going to start a war in Troy to get my brother's wife back! CHARGE! *(exits waving sword)*

**CHORUS 1:** Atreus' sons in vengeful ire, 'gainst Paris. But, he insulted the goddess Artemis, by boasting he was a better hunter than her. What hubris!

*(enter AGAMEMNON)*

**AGAMEMNON:** Artemis has stopped the winds, so I can not sail. I now must pay a hefty price. *(exits dejected)*

**CHORUS 1:** The only way to recover the winds was to sacrifice his daughter, Iphigenia. His child to slay and with her spilt blood make an offering to Artemis.

*(scream from backstage)*

**CHORUS 1:** The queen was sooo mad at him!

**CLYTEMNESTRA:** *(enters with servants)* Nothing worse than a woman scorned! I need to plot my vengeance! *(yells)* Evil boyfriend, get out here!

*(enter AEGISTHUS)*

**AEGISTHUS:** You called, my love? *(they huddle and plot)*

**CHORUS 1:** *(whispers)* They plotted to kill Agamemnon upon his return. Speaking of... Queen Clytemnestra, speak and say what messenger of joy today? Is there news of the war?

**CLYTEMNESTRA:** Troy is ours! The war is won!

*(CHORUS cheers; TOWNSPEOPLE enter)*

**CHORUS 1:** Look, out of darkness dawns a light. Agamemnon has returned!

*(AEGISTHUS sneaks off as AGAMEMNON, CASSANDRA, and SOLDIERS enter; ALL bow)*

**AGAMEMNON:** What a war! We have made them pay for stealing Helen. Now to my palace and the shrines of home.

**CLYTEMNESTRA:** Oh, citizens of Argos! I will speak my love for my husband!

**CHORUS 1:** This should be good.

**CLYTEMNESTRA:** Ten long years I have waited! I sent our children away for their safety, which left me all alone to cry. ALL. ALONE. For me, long since the gushing fount of tears is swept away; no drop is left to shed.

**AGAMEMNON:** Sheesh, I get it. But, I was at war, not off playing video games! Again.

**CLYTEMNESTRA:** Whatever. Welcome home, husband! Servants, lay down the cloths so that my husband may walk upon them.

*(SERVANTS lay down purple cloth)*

**AGAMEMNON:** I don't think I should. A mortal man to set foot on those rich dyes? Sounds like hubris to me and we all know how that turned out last time.

**CLYTEMNESTRA:** Argos has tons of purple cloth lying around. Walk on the cloth, it's ok.

**AGAMEMNON:** Nah, I'm good.

**CLYTEMNESTRA:** I bet the other kings are walking on cloths right now. Are you not as great as they are?

**AGAMEMNON:** Ok, ok, sheesh! I'll walk on the cloths. *(walks on cloth)* By the way, this is Cassandra, princess of Troy. She is the prize and flower of all we won.

**CLYTEMNESTRA:** She's your... flower?

**AGAMEMNON:** My reward. Elders, take care of her, I'm off to my palace. *(AGAMEMNON exits with SOLDIERS)*

**CLYTEMNESTRA:** Zeus, let me have my revenge! *(looks upward)* LIKE NOW!!!

**CHORUS 1:** Oh my! That's not good. Look at her evil glare!

**CLYTEMNESTRA:** Hey, Cassandra! *(pause)* Do you hear me?

*(CASSANDRA stares off)*

**CLYTEMNESTRA:** Yo, flower girl. Get inside! *(to audience)* She had better stay out of my way. No one ever accused me of having a green thumb, if you know what I mean. *(evil laugh)*

*(CASSANDRA still staring)*

**CLYTEMNESTRA:** *(to CHORUS)* Does she understand me? Helloooooo!

**CHORUS 1:** *(to CASSANDRA)* You should probably listen to her.

*(CASSANDRA continues staring)*

**CLYTEMNESTRA**: I don't have time for this! The Elders can deal with you. *(ALL exit, except CHORUS and CASSANDRA)*

**CASSANDRA**: Apollo! God of all ways, but only Death's to me.

**CHORUS 1**: She speaks! But I have no idea what she says. *(CHORUS shrugs)*

**CASSANDRA**: Apollo, your curse has led me from one horror to another! You gave me the gift of seeing, but not being believed.

**CHORUS 1**: She says she is a prophet! Maybe she knows something we don't. *(to CASSANDRA)* Do you know where you are? You're at Agamemnon's palace.

**CASSANDRA**: *(frantic)* No! This is a house of despair! It is cursed! *(has a vision)* A bath, a trap! She smites him!

**CHORUS 1**: Yep! She's crazy.

**CASSANDRA**: The King will be killed! I will also die! But an avenger will come!

**CHORUS 1**: Iron Man? *(looks at audience)* What? I'm a big fan.

**CASSANDRA**: I was right about the fall of Troy and I'm right about this. No one ever believes me. *(cries)*

**CHORUS 1**: There, there. I believe you. *(shakes head to audience)*

**CASSANDRA**: I wish Apollo never gave me this "gift." *(exits crying)*

**AGAMEMNON:** *(screams from offstage)* I am murdered! *(CHORUS gasp; AGAMEMNON runs onstage)* Murdered! Oh, they got me while I was in the bath! Not cool! Isn't anyone coming to save me? *(CLYTEMNESTRA enters, pulls AGAMEMNON offstage while screaming)* O I am sped - a deep, a moral blow!

**CHORUS 1:** Oh dear, the king has been killed!

**CLYTEMNESTRA:** *(enters triumphantly)* Finally, vengeance for my murdered child, Iphigenia.

**CHORUS 1:** Bless you.

**CLYTEMNESTRA:** And I had help from my secret boyfriend, Aegisthus. Isn't that right, honey?

**AEGISTHUS:** *(enters)* That's right! I am Agamemnon's cousin and I also wanted him dead! His dad killed my brothers and secretly served them to my father for dinner!

**CHORUS 1:** I'm gonna be sick. *(retching, runs off stage)*

**AEGISTHUS:** Dawn of the day of rightful vengeance!

**CLYTEMNESTRA:** I also got rid of that annoying Cassandra. No one ignores me, flower or not!

**CASSANDRA:** *(enters)* Wait, I'm dead already? The play just started.

**CLYTEMNESTRA:** I suppose you should have SEEN it coming. Bye, bye, Petunia.

*(CASSANDRA falls over dead)*

**CLYTEMNESTRA**: *(to AEGISTHUS)* I and thou will rule the palace. *(they exit)*

*(CHORUS 1 returns)*

**CHORUS 1**: Wow. Cassandra was right.

**CASSANDRA**: FINALLY! Someone believes me! *(dies again)*

**CHORUS 1**: There, there, child. *(to audience)* But, remember, she said there would be an avenger. *(looks at audience member)* What did you say? Did you say, Thor? Well, he is a god AND an avenger. Let's go on to the second play and find out!

*(ALL exit)*

## Act Two - The Libation Bearers

Outside Argos, the tomb of Agamemnon

*(Someone walks by with a sign that says, "PLAY 2 - The Libation Bearers. Several years later"; enter ORESTES)*

**ORESTES:** After all these years, me, who from banishment returning, stand on this, my country and my father's grave.

*(enter ELECTRA carrying libations and followed by CHORUS)*

**ORESTES:** I see Electra, mine own sister with her servant approaching my father's grave! I wonder what they are doing?

*(ORESTES hides and watches)*

**CHORUS 2:** *(to audience)* We have been sent by Clytemnestra to bring libations for the dead.

**ELECTRA:** *(to CHORUS)* This offering is a tribute to my father. But, it comes from his killer, my mother. Please, counsel me!

**CHORUS 2:** Awkward. Pray for Orestes to return and avenge your father's death.

**ELECTRA:** Great idea! *(speaks to gods)* I ask for Orestes, who shall the slayer slay. There, that should do it!

*(ORESTES comes out of hiding)*

**ORESTES:** I am he, Orestes, and I have come to avenge my father!

**CHORUS 2:** Wow, that was fast! *(to audience)* He's no Thor, though.

**ELECTRA:** How did you know to come?

**ORESTES**: The oracle of Apollo told me I must come and avenge my father, or the Gods would punish me with horrible diseases, wreaking their wrath on me.

**CHORUS 2**: Yuck!

**ELECTRA**: Well, last night, mom had a terror of a dream that she gave birth to a snake, and it bit her. She totally freaked, then sent us to offer libations so the gods don't punish her.

**ORESTES**: This dream - it bodes a man's revenge! I am that snake!

**CHORUS 2**: Okaaaaay. Weirdo.

**ORESTES**: Just, go inside and act normal.

*(ELECTRA and CHORUS nod and exit; ORESTES knocks on door)*

**ORESTES**: Hello? Anyone home?

**CLYTEMNESTRA**: *(entering)* Oh, I hope it's not Artemis trying to get me to join her hunters again. Oh good, it's just some random guy. *(to ORESTES)* What do you want, stranger?

**ORESTES**: Stranger? Yes! I am a stranger, with a message for you. Your son, Orestes, is no more. Sorry. Dead. Bummer.

**CLYTEMNESTRA**: No! That can't be! You had better come in.

*(CLYTEMNESTRA and ORESTES exit; CHORUS enters)*

**CHORUS 2**: It's obvious the queen is pretending to be sad... but I know she is happy her son is dead. I know, I know... his own mother! But, with Orestes gone, she would remain on the throne. What villainy! Wait! I hear Aegisthus, now.

**AEGISTHUS**: *(backstage if doubling roles with ORESTES)* Help, help, alas!

**CHORUS 2**: Oh, it sounds as if Orestes figured out Clytemnestra's plot.

**CLYTEMNESTRA**: *(runs onstage)* Orestes has killed Aegisthus! *(dramatically)* My lord is done to death!

*(ORESTES enters with AEGISTHUS, if not doubling roles, who shrugs and dies)*

**CLYTEMNESTRA**: *(sobbing)* No, not my love!

**ORESTES**: What, lov'st the man? Then in his grave lie down.

**CLYTEMNESTRA**: Well... I may not have loved him THAT much... Wait! It's YOU! Take pity on your mother! I gave birth to you!

**ORESTES**: Hmmm, that is true. *(to CHORUS)* What should I do? I'm confused! Should I spare my mother?

**CHORUS 2**: Well, Apollo did foretell this at Delphi. You probably don't want to make him mad. Being a god and all.

**ORESTES:** Soooo, choose between my mom or a god that will strike me down with a horrendous disease?

**CHORUS 2:** Right!

**ORESTES:** Ok, then. You chose THAT man over my father, I will slay thee at his side.

**CLYTEMNESTRA:** WHAT?! Ummm... your father did sacrifice your sister, remember?

**ORESTES:** He was fighting in a war while you plotted his death with another man!

**CLYTEMNESTRA:** Well, he was gone an awfully long time. 'Tis hard for wives to live as widows, child.

**ORESTES:** No excuses! I am the snake in your dream!

**CHORUS 2:** Wow, he's really gonna do it. That's got to be bad karma.

*(ORESTES kills CLYTEMNESTRA)*

**ORESTES:** Here are the tyrants who killed my father and stole the crown. I say that rightfully I slew my mother. *(sounding a bit crazy)* The gods would never punish me for this, right?

**CHORUS 2:** I think he's losing it.

**ORESTES:** *(crazier)* They were bad people! Apollo told me to do it!

**CHORUS 2**: Yep, insane in the membrane.

**ORESTES**: *(and crazier)* I must away!

**CHORUS 2**: Good idea. Go on a nice little trip… away from here.

**ORESTES**: Do you guys see those ghosts? *(pointing offstage)*

**CHORUS 2**: He needs some serious therapy. I know, go seek help from Apollo! *(shoves ORESTES offstage)*

**ORESTES**: *(yelling)* Apollo!

**CHORUS 2**: *(to audience)* Don't worry, the play doesn't end like this. Remember, this is a trilogy. There's one play left. Thank the gods.

*(ALL exit)*

## Act Three - The Eumenides

*(someone walks by with a sign that says, "Play 3 - The Eumenides - Several days later"; CHORUS and ORESTES enter; CHORUS chanting around ORESTES; APOLLO enters)*

**APOLLO:** SLEEP! *(CHORUS and ORESTES sleep)* Whew, I'm glad that fury is quiet. She better not wake up. Nothing like the goddess of vengeance to ruin your day. *(notices audience)* Oh! Well, hello! Welcome to Delphi and the temple of... me! You know, Apollo. The coolest god around. Anyway, time to help my little buddy here. *(whispering)* Orestes!

**ORESTES:** *(sadly)* What?

**APOLLO:** I know for by my hest thou didst thy mother slay. But, wow, I didn't think you'd actually do it! That was entertaining!

**ORESTES:** Entertaining? *(to the audience)* Talk about mixed messages.

**APOLLO:** Listen, go to Athens and the goddess Athena will give you a trial. I'll put in a good word for you. She's my half sister, and she loves me. Well, everybody loves me. I got your back, bro.

**ORESTES:** Yeah, ok. If you say so... bro. *(exits, APOLLO exits opposite)*

**CLYTEMNESTRA:** *(enters)* The wandering ghost that once was Clytemnestra calls - Arise! *(CHORUS doesn't move)* My own son killed me! ARISE!!! *(CHORUS rises)* While you were sleeping, he got away! Go after him!

*(CHORUS standing and ready to fight; CLYTEMNESTRA exits; APOLLO enters)*

**APOLLO:** Are you still here? Out! I command you!

**CHORUS 3**: This is all your fault. Thine oracle bade this man slay his mother. Not cool!

**APOLLO**: Chill out. I simply said to avenge a wife who slays her lord.

**CHORUS 3**: I followed him all the way here, and there are no planes in Ancient Greece. I had to walk! I loathe walking!

**APOLLO**: Waah! Why were you bothering Orestes, but not Clytemnestra? She killed her husband!

**CHORUS 3**: He wasn't her blood. Plus Agamemnon was kind of a meanie. I will haunt Orestes forever for killing his mom.

**APOLLO**: *(mocking CHORUS)* I will haunt Orestes forever... Whatever. If you want him so badly, follow then!! But, I do like him, so I will save him. Oh, and guess what? I CAN fly. Smell ya later! *(APOLLO exits with a flurry)*

**CHORUS 3**: Ohhh... I REALLY don't like that guy!!! Ah man, I have to walk again?! Ugh...

*(CHORUS exits; someone walks by with a sign that says, "Outside the temple of Athena in Athens")*

**ORESTES**: *(enters and kneels)* I call Athena, lady of this land. Apollo told me I should come stand trial. Please be merciful.

*(CHORUS enters)*

**CHORUS 3**: There he is. Finally! My feet are killing me!

**ORESTES**: Oh no, you again? You're so... creepy. Look, I'm pretty sure Athena will take pity on me and Apollo is totally on my side.

**CHORUS 3:** Thee, not Apollo nor Athena's strength, can save from perishing. And DON'T run again! I'm tired! *(CHORUS does a wild magical gesture toward ORESTES, who freezes in place)* Sweet! I rock!

*(ATHENA enters)*

**ATHENA:** What mischief abounds? Who are ye?

**CHORUS 3:** Goddess Athena! I am a child of eternal night, and a fury in the underworld. I've been haunting this dude for pages now.

**ATHENA:** Oh, the vengeance lady. What hath this insignificant mortal done?

**CHORUS 3:** He did his mother slay.

**ATHENA:** Hmmm... I suppose that could be bad. But, why?

**CHORUS 3:** Well... she did kill his dad.

**ATHENA:** A conundrum! Too mighty is this matter. I know! We shall have a trial! I, of course, shall be judge, because, well, I AM the goddess of wisdom. And we will have a jury of Athenians. If I can find any backstage. *(exits)*

**CHORUS 3:** Seriously, a trial? So boring! How about I "try" to rip him to pieces.

*(CHORUS creeps toward ORESTES; ATHENA enters; CHORUS acts innocent, unfreezes ORESTES)*

**ATHENA:** Ok, so, we are out of actors backstage. I know! Audience, YOU shall be our jury! Excellent idea, if I do say so myself! Let the trial begin.

*(EVERYONE takes their "court" positions; APOLLO enters)*

**CHORUS 3:** Apollo, why are you here?

**APOLLO:** I came to defend Orestes.

**CHORUS 3:** You're not a lawyer!

**APOLLO:** I'm a god!

**CHORUS 3:** That does sound like a lawyer.

**ATHENA:** Hello, brother.

**APOLLO:** Yo! What up, Thena!

**ATHENA:** Alright! Let's begin. Tell the tale first and set the matter clear.

**CHORUS 3:** Orestes, hast then thy mother slain??

**ORESTES:** I slew her. I deny no word hereof.

**CHORUS 3:** I rest my case.

**ORESTES:** Wait! I killed her, but Apollo told me to. Plus, she killed my father.

**CHORUS 3:** But, she was not kin by blood to him she slew.

**ORESTES:** Huh?

**CHORUS 3:** It's way worse to kill someone of your own blood.

**ORESTES:** Ohhhh.

**APOLLO:** *(to ORESTES)* I got this, bro. *(to the audience)* She was only his mom. The male is the parent! She was just a... a woman.

*(EVERYONE gasps)*

**CHORUS 3:** What?!

**ORESTES:** *(to APOLLO)* Dude, I'm not sure that's the best defense.

**APOLLO:** Shhh... That he should die, a chieftain, and a king... by female hands! Shameful.

**ATHENA:** Ok, enough is said. Fury, do you rest your case?

**CHORUS:** Yes.

**ATHENA:** Apollo, do you rest your case?

**APOLLO:** *(looking at himself in a mirror)* What? Yeah, sure.

**ATHENA:** *(to audience)* Citizens of Athens, we had our first trial! Well, go ahead, applaud for me. *(coax audience to applaud)* Wow, I'm super smart! So, since you are also the jury, have you come to a decision? *(waiting impatiently)* Oh my gods, you people are worthless! Hmmm, well mine is the right to add the final vote. I say Orestes will go free! I like him. He's cute.

*(CHORUS pouts; ORESTES and APOLLO high five)*

**APOLLO:** I'm good at this lawyering stuff.

**ORESTES:** Wow! I was pretty sure that fury was going to rip me to pieces.

**CHORUS:** I still can!

**ORESTES:** Ok, then... I will return to rule Argos. And now farewell thou and thy city's folk. And especially you! *(points to CHORUS)*

*(APOLLO and ORESTES exit)*

**CHORUS 3:** Well that stinks. Now I don't know what to do. Nothing with Apollo, that's for sure! That guy's a pig!

**ATHENA**: Fury, be appeased. You mighty deity shall stay in Athens. You can help good people and punish the bad. Instead of just punishing all the time.

**CHORUS 3**: That doesn't sound too bad, and no more walking!

**ATHENA**: You will be known as The Eumenides.

**CHORUS 3**: The what now?

**ATHENA**: The Eumenides. It means "the kindly ones".

**CHORUS 3**: That's what that means! *(to the audience)* Alright people, who's been good... and who's been naughty?

*(CHORUS run offstage; ATHENA follows shaking her head)*

## THE END

# The 20-Minute or so
# THE ORESTEIA
# for Kids

by Aeschylus
Creatively modified by
Amanda Ruby & Brendan P. Kelso
## 10-19 Actors

### CAST OF CHARACTERS:

[1]**CHORUS 1:** Elder of Argos
[2]**CHORUS 2:** Elder of Argos
[1]**CHORUS 3:** Servant
[2]**CHORUS 4:** Servant
[1]**CHORUS 5:** Fury
[2]**CHORUS 6:** Fury
**CLYTEMNESTRA:** Wife of Agamemnon
[3]**MENELAUS:** Son of dead King
[6]**HELEN:** Helen of Troy, the most beautiful woman in the world
**AGAMEMNON:** Other son and King of Argos for a short period
[7]**KING PARIS:** King of Troy
[5]**CASSANDRA:** Princess of Troy
[4]**AEGISTHUS:** Clytemnestra's secret boyfriend, Agamemnon's cousin
[7]**ORESTES:** Son of Clytemnestra and Agamemnon
[6]**ELECTRA:** Daughter of Clytemnestra and Agamemnon
[5]**NURSE:** Clytemnestra's nurse - a talented actress!

[3]**APOLLO:** self-absorbed God of the Sun, Music, and other cool things
**ATHENA:** Goddess of Wisdom
[4]**JUROR:** a juror

Characters with no lines:
Soldiers/Guards/Servants/Jurors

[1]Same actor can play CHORUS 1, 3, and 5
[2]Same actor can play CHORUS 2, 4, and 6
[3]Same actor can play MENELAUS and APOLLO
[4]Same actor can play AEGISTHUS and JUROR
[5]Same actor can play CASSANDRA and NURSE
[6]Same actor can play HELEN and ELECTRA
[7]Same actor can play PARIS and ORESTES
*anyone not on stage can play extra Soldiers/Guards/Servants/Jurors

## ACT 1 - Agamemnon

*(Someone walks by with a sign that says, "PLAY 1 - AGAMEMNON"; CHORUS enters)*

**CHORUS 1:** I hope we hear news of the war soon. Ten livelong years have rolled away since the Trojan War began.

**CHORUS 2:** Yes, this mess of a kingdom, Argos, needs some good news for once.

**CHORUS 1:** *(to audience)* As elders, we know all the stories. Long ago, King Atreus was murdered by his brother.

*(enter AGAMEMNON and MENELAUS)*

**MENELAUS:** No, Dad!!!

**CHORUS 2:** Then his sons, Agamemnon and Menelaus, fled to Sparta.

**AGAMEMNON:** We have to flee or we're next!

*(AGAMEMNON and MENELAUS exit screaming)*

**CHORUS 1:** Where the King of Sparta let Agamemnon marry his daughter, Clytemnestra.

*(enter AGAMEMNON and CLYTEMNESTRA)*

**AGAMEMNON:** I do!

**CLYTEMNESTRA:** I do, too!

*(AGAMEMNON and CLYTEMNESTRA exit)*

**CHORUS:** Awwwwe.

**CHORUS 2:** *(sniffling)* I always cry at weddings.

**CHORUS 1:** Then Menelaus became King of Sparta when their king died.

*(enter MENELAUS wearing crown)*

**MENELAUS:** I am the King of Sparta!

**CHORUS 2:** He also got to marry the king's other daughter, Helen, who is the most beautiful woman in the world.

*(enter HELEN)*

**HELEN:** I am. Let's go dear.

*(MENELAUS and HELEN exit holding hands)*

**CHORUS 1:** Agamemnon returned from Sparta, killed his uncle, and reclaimed the throne!

**CHORUS 2:** Oh, just like Hamlet, no wait, Lion King!

**CHORUS 1:** No, no no! Those stories were based on this story!

**CHORUS 2:** Cool!

**CHORUS 1:** So that's kind of how this current war got started. You see, a few years later, King Paris of Troy stopped in for a not-so-friendly visit.

*(HELEN enters; PARIS enters opposite)*

**PARIS:** You are the one Aphrodite promised me.

**HELEN:** I am?

**PARIS:** You shall come with me.

**HELEN:** I will?

*(PARIS takes HELEN by the wrist and leads her offstage)*

**HELEN:** HELP!!! Stranger danger!!!

**CHORUS 2:** They returned to Troy. Menelaus and his brother Agamemnon, Atreus' sons in vengeful ire, 'gainst Paris, started a war to get her back.

*(enter AGAMEMNON and MENELAUS)*

**AGAMEMNON:** Let's get your wife back!

**AGAMEMNON & MENELAUS:** Charge! *(both exit)*

**CHORUS 1:** But, King Agamemnon made a fatal error.

**CHORUS 2:** He insulted the goddess Artemis, by boasting he was a better hunter than her. What hubris!

**CHORUS 1:** Artemis stopped the winds so he could not sail. The only way to recover was to sacrifice his daughter, Iphigenia. His child to slay and with her spilt blood make an offering to Artemis.

*(scream heard backstage)*

**CHORUS 2:** Dark.

**CHORUS 1:** The queen was sooo mad at him!

**CLYTEMNESTRA:** *(enters with servants)* Nothing worse than a woman scorned!

**CHORUS 2:** *(whispers)* So mad she got a boyfriend while he was gone. Together, they plotted to kill Agamemnon upon his return. Speaking of...

**CHORUS 1:** Queen Clytemnestra, speak and say what messenger of joy today? Is there news of the war?

**CLYTEMNESTRA:** Troy is ours! The war is won!

*(CHORUS cheers; TOWNSPEOPLE enter)*

**CHORUS 2:** Look, out of darkness dawns a light. Agamemnon has returned!

*(enter AGAMEMNON, CASSANDRA, and SOLDIERS; ALL bow)*

**AGAMEMNON:** What a war! We have made them pay for stealing Helen. Now to my palace and the shrines of home.

**CLYTEMNESTRA:** Oh, citizens of Argos! I will speak my love for my husband!

**CHORUS 1:** This should be good.

**CLYTEMNESTRA:** Ten long years I have waited! I sent our children away for their safety, which left me all alone to cry. ALL. ALONE. For me, long since the gushing fount of tears is swept away; no drop is left to shed.

**AGAMEMNON:** Sheesh, I get it. But, I was at war, not off playing video games! Again.

**CLYTEMNESTRA:** Whatever. Welcome home, husband! Servants, lay down the cloths so that my husband may walk upon them.

*(SERVANTS lay down purple cloth)*

**AGAMEMNON:** I don't think I should. A mortal man to set foot on those rich dyes? Sounds like hubris to me and we all know how that turned out last time.

**CLYTEMNESTRA:** Argos has tons of purple cloth lying around. Walk on the cloth, it's ok.

**AGAMEMNON:** Nah, I'm good.

**CLYTEMNESTRA:** I bet the other kings are walking on cloths right now. Are you not as great as they are?

**AGAMEMNON:** Ok, ok, sheesh! I'll walk on the cloths. *(walks on cloth)* By the way, this is Cassandra, princess of Troy. She is the prize and flower of all we won.

**CLYTEMNESTRA:** She's your... flower?

**AGAMEMNON:** My reward. Elders, take care of her, I'm off to my palace. *(AGAMEMNON exits with SOLDIERS)*

**CLYTEMNESTRA:** Zeus, let me have my revenge! *(looks upward)* LIKE NOW!!!

**CHORUS 2:** I've got a bad feeling about this.

**CHORUS 1:** Wow! Look at her evil glare!

**CLYTEMNESTRA:** Hey, Cassandra! *(pause)* Do you hear me?

*(CASSANDRA stares off)*

**CLYTEMNESTRA:** Yo, flower girl. Get inside! *(to audience)* She had better stay out of my way. No one ever accused me of having a green thumb, if you know what I mean. *(evil laugh)*

*(CASSANDRA still staring)*

**CLYTEMNESTRA:** *(to CHORUS)* Does she understand me? Helloooooo!

**CHORUS 2:** *(to CASSANDRA)* You should probably listen to her.

*(CASSANDRA continues staring)*

**CLYTEMNESTRA:** I don't have time for this! The Elders can deal with you. *(ALL exit, except CHORUS and CASSANDRA)*

**CASSANDRA:** Apollo! God of all ways, but only Death's to me.

**CHORUS 1:** She speaks! But I have no idea what she says. *(CHORUS shrugs)*

**CASSANDRA:** Apollo, your curse has led me from one horror to another! You gave me the gift of seeing, but not being believed.

**CHORUS 2:** *(aside to other CHORUS)* Maybe she's mad.

**CHORUS 1:** She says she is a prophet! Maybe she knows something we don't. *(to CASSANDRA)* Do you know where you are? You're at Agamemnon's palace.

**CASSANDRA:** *(frantic)* No! This is a house of despair! It is cursed! *(has a vision)* A bath, a trap! She smites him!

**CHORUS 2:** Yep! She's mad.

**CASSANDRA:** The King will be killed! I will also die! But an avenger will come!

**CHORUS 1:** Iron Man? *(CHORUS glares)* What? I'm a big fan.

**CASSANDRA:** I was right about the fall of Troy and I'm right about this. No one ever believes me. *(cries)*

**CHORUS 2:** There, there. We believe you, don't we?

*(CHORUS mumbles and shrugs, looks at her like she's crazy)*

**CASSANDRA:** I wish Apollo never gave me this "gift." *(exits crying)*

**AGAMEMNON:** *(screams from offstage)* I am murdered! *(CHORUS gasp; AGAMEMNON runs onstage)* Murdered! Oh, they got me while I was in the bath! Not cool! Isn't anyone coming to save me? *(CLYTEMNESTRA enters, pulls AGAMEMNON offstage while screaming)* O I am sped - a deep, a moral blow!

**CHORUS 1:** I think the king has been killed!

**CHORUS 2:** Ya think?? What should we do?

**CHORUS 1:** Sit back and watch, this is entertaining! *(nods for audience's agreement)*

**CLYTEMNESTRA:** *(enters triumphantly)* Finally, vengeance for my murdered child, Iphigenia.

**CHORUS 2:** Bless you.

**CLYTEMNESTRA:** And I had help from my secret boyfriend, Aegisthus. Isn't that right, honey?

**AEGISTHUS:** *(enters)* That's right! I am Agamemnon's cousin and I also wanted him dead! His dad killed my brothers and secretly served them to my father for dinner!

**CHORUS 1:** It's Titus Andronicus! You sure Shakespeare didn't write this?

**CHORUS 2:** I'm gonna be sick. *(retching, runs off stage)*

**AEGISTHUS:** Dawn of the day of rightful vengeance!

**CLYTEMNESTRA:** I also got rid of that annoying Cassandra. No one ignores me, flower or not!

**CASSANDRA:** *(enters)* Wait, I'm dead already? The play just started.

**CLYTEMNESTRA:** I suppose you should have SEEN it coming. Bye, bye, Petunia.

*(CASSANDRA falls over dead)*

**CLYTEMNESTRA:** *(to AEGISTHUS)* I and thou will rule the palace. *(exits with AEGISTHUS)*

*(CHORUS 2 returns)*

**CHORUS 1:** Wow. Cassandra was right.

**CASSANDRA:** FINALLY! Someone believes me! *(dies again)*

**CHORUS 2:** This sure is one crazy family!

**CHORUS 1:** But, remember, she said there would be an avenger?

**CHORUS 2:** Thor, right? He's an avenger AND a god.

*(CHORUS glares again)*

**CHORUS 1:** I bet Agamemnon's son will return and avenge his father's death!

**CHORUS 2:** Oh, yeah! Orestes, I forgot about him!

**CHORUS 1:** Well, this whole trilogy is kind of named after him.

*(CHORUS mumbles in agreement)*

*(ALL exit)*

# Act Two - The Libation Bearers

Outside Argos, the tomb of Agamemnon

*(Someone walks by with a sign that says, "PLAY 2 - The Libation Bearers. Several years later"; enter ORESTES)*

**ORESTES:** After all these years, me, who from banishment returning, stand on this, my country and my father's grave.

*(enter ELECTRA carrying libations and followed by CHORUS)*

**ORESTES:** I see Electra, mine own sister with her servants approaching my father's grave! I wonder what they are doing?

*(ORESTES hides and watches)*

**CHORUS 3:** *(to audience)* We have been sent by Clytemnestra to bring libations for the dead.

**CHORUS 4:** She's trying to make up for the fact that she murdered her husband! *(motions to ELECTRA)* HER dad.

**CHORUS 3:** Awkward!

**ELECTRA:** *(to CHORUS)* This offering is a tribute to my father. But, it comes from his killer, my mother. Please, counsel me!

**CHORUS 4:** Pray for Orestes to return and avenge your father's death.

**ELECTRA:** Great idea! *(speaks to gods)* I ask for Orestes, who shall the slayer slay. There, that should do it!

*(ORESTES comes out of hiding)*

**ORESTES:** I am he, Orestes, and I have come to avenge my father!

**CHORUS 3:** Wow, that was fast! *(to audience)* He's no Thor, though.

**ELECTRA:** How did you know to come?

**ORESTES:** The oracle of Apollo told me I must come and avenge my father, or the Gods would punish me with horrible diseases, wreaking their wrath on me.

**CHORUS 4:** Yuck!

**ELECTRA:** Well, last night, mom had a terror of a dream that she gave birth to a snake, and it bit her. She totally freaked, then sent us to offer libations so the gods don't punish her.

**ORESTES:** This dream - it bodes a man's revenge! I am that snake!

**CHORUS 3:** Okaaaaay. Weirdo.

**ORESTES:** Just, go inside and act normal.

*(ELECTRA and CHORUS nod and exit; ORESTES knocks on door)*

**ORESTES:** Hello? Anyone home?

**CLYTEMNESTRA:** *(entering)* Oh, I hope it's not Artemis trying to get me to join her hunters again. Oh good, it's just some random guy. *(to ORESTES)* What do you want, stranger?

**ORESTES:** Stranger? Yes! I am a stranger, with a message for you. Your son, Orestes, is no more. Sorry. Dead. Bummer.

**CLYTEMNESTRA:** No! That can't be! You had better come in.

*(CLYTEMNESTRA and ORESTES exit; CHORUS enters)*

**CHORUS 4:** I hope Orestes knows what he's doing.

**CHORUS 3:** Look, here comes Orestes' nurse. She's crying.

**NURSE:** The Queen ordered me to get Aegisthus so that he can hear the news himself.

**CHORUS 4:** Is the queen upset?

**NURSE:** She is pretending to be sad... but I know she is happy her son is dead.

**CHORUS 3:** *(shaking her head)* His own mother!

**CHORUS 4:** With no male heir of Agamemnon left, they remain on the throne.

**NURSE:** But I truly am sad. I cared for Orestes since birth, and now he's dead. Well, I guess I'll go fetch Aegisthus.

**CHORUS 3:** Wait, are you to tell Aegisthus to bring henchmen or to come alone?

**NURSE:** The queen bids him bring a spear-armed bodyguard.

**CHORUS 4:** Maybe, leave that part out.

**NURSE:** *(shrugs)* OK. *(exits)*

**CHORUS 3:** Look, here comes Aegisthus.

**AEGISTHUS:** *(enters)* I heard a traveler arrived with a new rumor. Orestes is dead?

**CHORUS 4:** *(shrugs)* Dunno. Why don't you go inside and find out?

**AEGISTHUS:** I shall! *(exits; pause; screams)* Help, help, alas!

**NURSE:** *(runs onstage)* Someone has killed Aegisthus! *(dramatically)* My lord is done to death! *(calmly)* See, I can pretend to be upset, too.

*(CHORUS applaud, NURSE curtsies)*

**CLYTEMNESTRA:** *(enters)* What's with all the shouting?

**NURSE:** My Queen, Aegisthus has been killed.

**CLYTEMNESTRA:** What?!? No!

*(NURSE exits; ORESTES enters with AEGISTHUS who shrugs and dies)*

**CLYTEMNESTRA:** *(sobbing)* No, not my love!

**ORESTES:** What, lov'st the man? Then in his grave lie down.

**CLYTEMNESTRA:** Well... I may not have loved him THAT much... Wait! It's YOU! Take pity on your mother! I gave birth to you!

**ORESTES:** Hmmm, that is true. *(to CHORUS)* What should I do? I'm confused! Should I spare my mother?

**CHORUS 3:** Well, Apollo did foretell this at Delphi. You probably don't want to make him mad. Being a god and all.

**ORESTES:** Soooo, choose between my mom or a god that will strike me down with a horrendous disease?

**CHORUS 4:** Right!

**ORESTES:** Ok, then. *(leads Clytemnestra to Aegisthus)* You chose him over my father, I will slay thee at his side.

**CLYTEMNESTRA:** WHAT?! Ummm... your father did sacrifice your sister, remember?

**ORESTES:** He was fighting in a war while you plotted his death with another man!

**CLYTEMNESTRA:** Well, he was gone an awfully long time. 'Tis hard for wives to live as widows, child.

**ORESTES:** No excuses! I am the snake in your dream!

**CHORUS 3:** Wow, he's really gonna do it.

**CHORUS 4:** That's got to be bad karma.

*(ORESTES kills CLYTEMNESTRA)*

**ORESTES:** Here are the tyrants who killed my father and stole the crown. I say that rightfully I slew my mother. *(sounding a bit crazy)* The gods would never punish me for this, right?

**CHORUS 3:** I think he's losing it.

**ORESTES:** *(crazier)* They were bad people! Apollo told me to do it!

**CHORUS 4:** Yep, insane in the membrane.

**ORESTES:** *(and crazier)* I must away!

**CHORUS 3:** Good idea. Go on a nice little trip... away from here.

**ORESTES:** Do you guys see those ghosts? *(pointing offstage)*

**CHORUS 4:** He needs some serious therapy.

**CHORUS 3:** Go to Apollo! *(shoves ORESTES offstage)*

**CHORUS 4:** Wait, the play doesn't end like this, does it? This is a mess!

**CHORUS 3:** Remember, this is a trilogy. There's one more play left.

**CHORUS 4:** Oh yeah! Thank the gods.

*(ALL exit)*

## Act Three - The Eumenides

*(someone walks by with a sign that says, "Play 3 - The Eumenides - Several days later"; CHORUS and ORESTES enter; CHORUS chanting, surround ORESTES; APOLLO enters)*

**APOLLO:** SLEEP! *(CHORUS and ORESTES sleep)* Whew, I'm glad those furies are quiet. They better not wake up. Nothing like the goddesses of vengeance to ruin your day. *(notices audience)* Oh! Well, hello! Welcome to Delphi and the temple of... me! You know, Apollo. The coolest god around. Anyway, time to help my little buddy here. *(whispering)* Orestes!

**ORESTES:** *(sadly)* What?

**APOLLO:** I know for by my hest thou didst thy mother slay. But, wow, I didn't think you'd actually do it! That was entertaining!

**ORESTES:** Entertaining? *(to the audience)* Talk about mixed messages.

**APOLLO:** Listen, go to Athens and the goddess Athena will give you a trial. I'll put in a good word for you. She's my half sister, and she loves me. Well, everybody loves me. I got your back, bro.

**ORESTES:** Yeah, ok. If you say so... bro. *(exits, APOLLO exits opposite)*

**CLYTEMNESTRA:** *(enters)* The wandering ghost that once was Clytemnestra calls - Arise! *(CHORUS doesn't move)* My own son killed me! ARISE!!! *(CHORUS rises)* While you furies were sleeping, he got away! Go after him!

*(CHORUS standing and ready to fight; CLYTEMNESTRA exits; APOLLO enters)*

**APOLLO:** Are you gals still here? Out! I command you!

**CHORUS 6**: This is all your fault. Thine oracle bade this man slay his mother.

**CHORUS 5**: Not cool!

**APOLLO**: Chill out. I simply said to avenge a wife who slays her lord.

**CHORUS 6**: We followed him all the way here, and there are no planes in Ancient Greece. We had to walk! I loathe walking!

**APOLLO**: Waah! Why were you bothering Orestes, but not Clytemnestra? She killed her husband!

**CHORUS 5**: He wasn't her blood. Plus Agamemnon was kind of a meanie.

**CHORUS 6**: We will haunt Orestes forever for killing his mom.

**APOLLO**: *(mocking CHORUS)* We will haunt Orestes forever... Whatever. If you want him so badly, follow then!! But, I do like him, so I will save him. Oh, and guess what? I CAN fly. Smell ya later! *(APOLLO exits with a flurry)*

**CHORUS 5**: Ohhh... I REALLY don't like that guy!!!

**CHORUS 6**: We have to walk again?! Ugh...

*(CHORUS exits; someone walks by with a sign that says, "Outside the temple of Athena in Athens")*

**ORESTES**: *(enters and kneels)* I call Athena, lady of this land. Apollo told me I should come stand trial. Please be merciful.

*(CHORUS enters)*

**CHORUS 5**: There he is.

**CHORUS 6**: Finally! My feet are killing me!

**ORESTES:** Oh no, you gals again? Look, I'm pretty sure Athena will take pity on me and Apollo is totally on my side.

**CHORUS 5:** Thee, not Apollo nor Athena's strength, can save from perishing.

**CHORUS 6:** Don't make him run again! I'm tired!

**CHORUS 5:** I've got an idea! Let's cast a binding spell so he can't move!

**CHORUS 6:** We can do that?

**CHORUS 5:** Ah, yeah. We're furies. We rock.

*(CHORUS does a wild magical gesture toward ORESTES, who freezes in place; CHORUS high fives; ATHENA enters)*

**ATHENA:** What mischief abounds? Who are ye?

**CHORUS 6:** Goddess Athena! We are the children of eternal night, and furies in the underworld. We've been haunting this dude for pages now.

**ATHENA:** Oh, the vengeance ladies. What hath this insignificant mortal done?

**CHORUS 5:** He did his mother slay.

**ATHENA:** Hmmm... I suppose that could be bad. But, why?

**CHORUS 6:** She did kill his dad.

**CHORUS 5:** Shhhh!

**ATHENA:** A conundrum! Too mighty is this matter. I know! We shall have a trial! I, of course, shall be judge, because, well, I AM the goddess of wisdom. And we will have a jury of Athenians. *(exits)*

**CHORUS 6:** Seriously, a trial? Boring!

**CHORUS 5:** Let's rip him to pieces.

**CHORUS 6:** Yessss!!!

*(CHORUS creeps toward ORESTES; ATHENA enters with JURY; CHORUS acts innocent, unfreezes ORESTES)*

**ATHENA:** Let the trial begin. Jury, stand over there.

*(EVERYONE takes their "court" positions; APOLLO enters)*

**CHORUS 6:** Apollo, why are you here?

**APOLLO:** I came to defend Orestes.

**CHORUS 5:** You're not a lawyer!

**APOLLO:** I'm a god!

**CHORUS 6:** That does sound like a lawyer.

**ATHENA:** Hello, brother.

**APOLLO:** Yo! What up, Thena!

**ATHENA:** Alright! Let's begin. Tell the tale first and set the matter clear.

**CHORUS 5:** Orestes, hast then thy mother slain??

**ORESTES:** I slew her. I deny no word hereof.

**CHORUS 6:** We rest our case.

**ORESTES:** Wait! I killed her, but Apollo told me to. Plus, she killed my father.

**CHORUS 5:** But, she was not kin by blood to him she slew.

**CHORUS 6:** Yeah, it's way worse to kill someone of your own blood.

**APOLLO:** *(to ORESTES)* I got this, bro. *(to the JURY)* She was only his mom. The male is the parent! She was just a... a woman.

*(EVERYONE gasps)*

**CHORUS 5:** Hold me back! *(CHORUS holds her back)*

**ORESTES:** *(to APOLLO)* Dude, I'm not sure that's the best defense.

**APOLLO:** Shhh... That he should die, a chieftain, and a king... by female hands! Shameful.

**ATHENA:** Ok, enough is said. Furies, do you rest your case?

**CHORUS:** Yes.

**ATHENA:** Apollo, do you rest your case?

**APOLLO:** *(looking at himself in a mirror)* What? Yeah, sure.

**ATHENA:** Jurors, make your decision.

*(JURY huddles)*

**ATHENA:** *(to audience)* Citizens of Athens, we had our first trial! Well, go ahead, applaud for me. *(coax audience to applaud)* Wow, I'm super smart! How's it going jury?

**JUROR:** It's a tie. We cannot agree.

**ATHENA:** Hmmm, well mine is the right to add the final vote. I say Orestes will go free! I like him. He's cute.

*(CHORUS pouts; ORESTES and APOLLO high five; JURY exits)*

**APOLLO:** I'm good at this lawyering stuff.

**ORESTES:** Wow! I was pretty sure those furies were going to rip me to pieces.

**CHORUS:** We still can!

**ORESTES:** Ok, then... I will return to rule Argos. And now farewell thou and thy city's folk. And especially you monsters! *(points to CHORUS)*

*(APOLLO and ORESTES exit)*

**CHORUS 6:** Well that stinks. We didn't even get to rip anyone to pieces.

**CHORUS 5:** What are we going to do now? Nothing with Apollo, that's for sure! That guy's a pig!

**ATHENA:** Ladies, be appeased. You mighty deities shall stay in Athens. You can help good people and punish the bad. Instead of just punishing all the time.

**CHORUS 6:** That doesn't sound too bad.

**CHORUS 5:** Yeah, and no more walking!

**ATHENA:** You will be known as The Eumenides.

**CHORUS 6:** The what now?

**ATHENA:** The Eumenides. It means "the kindly ones".

**CHORUS 6:** That's what that means!

**CHORUS 5:** I've been wondering this whole time.

**CHORUS 6:** *(to the audience)* Alright people, who's been good...

**CHORUS:** And who's been naughty?

*(CHORUS run offstage; ATHENA follows shaking her head)*

### THE END

# The 25-Minute or so THE ORESTEIA for Kids

by Aeschylus
Creatively modified by
Amanda Ruby & Brendan P. Kelso
**15-25 Actors**

### CAST OF CHARACTERS:

[1]**CHORUS 1**: Elder of Argos
[2]**CHORUS 2**: Elder of Argos
[3]**CHORUS 3**: Elder of Argos
[1]**CHORUS 4**: Servant
[2]**CHORUS 5**: Servant
[3]**CHORUS 6**: Servant
[1]**CHORUS 7**: Fury
[2]**CHORUS 8**: Fury
[3]**CHORUS 9**: Fury
**CLYTEMNESTRA**: Wife of Agamemnon
[4]**KING ATREUS**: King who dies
**MENELAUS**: Son of dead King
[7]**HELEN**: Helen of Troy, the most beautiful woman in the world
**AGAMEMNON**: Other son and King of Argos for a short period
[6]**ARTEMIS**: the wickedly awesome Goddess of the Hunt
[6]**A HERALD**: Someone who brings news and eats worms

**KING PARIS:** King of Troy
[5]**CASSANDRA:** Princess of Troy
**AEGISTHUS:** Clytemnestra's secret boyfriend, Agamemnon's cousin
**ORESTES:** Son of Clytemnestra and Agamemnon
[7]**ELECTRA:** Daughter of Clytemnestra and Agamemnon
[5]**NURSE:** Clytemnestra's nurse - a talented actress!
**APOLLO:** self-absorbed God of the Sun, Music, and other cool things
**ATHENA:** Goddess of Wisdom
[4]**JUROR:** a juror

Characters with no lines:
Soldiers/Guards/Servants/Jurors/Huntresses

[1]Same actor can play CHORUS 1, 4, and 7
[2]Same actor can play CHORUS 2, 5, and 8
[3]Same actor can play CHORUS 3, 6, and 9
[4]Same actor can play KING ATREUS and JUROR
[5]Same actor can play CASSANDRA and NURSE
[6]Same actor can play ARTEMIS and HERALD
[7]Same actor can play HELEN and ELECTRA
*anyone not on stage can play extra Soldiers/Guards/Servants/Jurors/Huntresses

## ACT 1 - Agamemnon

*(Someone walks by with a sign that says, "PLAY 1 - AGAMEMNON", CHORUS enters)*

**CHORUS 1:** I hope we hear news of the war soon. Ten livelong years have rolled away since the Trojan War began.

**CHORUS 2:** Yes, the kingdom of Argos needs some good news for once.

**CHORUS 3:** *(to audience)* How did we get in this mess, you ask? Well, as elders, we know all the stories. Long ago, King Atreus was murdered by his brother.

*(KING ATREUS enters and dies melodramatically)*

**CHORUS 1:** Then his sons, Agamemnon and Menelaus, fled to Sparta.

*(enter AGAMEMNON and MENELAUS)*

**MENELAUS:** No, Dad!!!

**KING ATREUS:** My brother killed me! Avenge meeeee!!!! *(dies again)*

**AGAMEMNON:** We have to flee or we're next!

*(AGAMEMNON and MENELAUS exit screaming)*

**CHORUS 2:** But, the boys got lucky. The King of Sparta let Agamemnon marry his daughter, Clytemnestra.

*(enter AGAMEMNON and CLYTEMNESTRA)*

**AGAMEMNON:** I do!

**CLYTEMNESTRA:** I do, too!

*(AGAMEMNON and CLYTEMNESTRA exit)*

**CHORUS:** Awwwwe.

**CHORUS 3:** *(sniffling)* I always cry at weddings.

**CHORUS 1:** Then Menelaus became King of Sparta when their king died.

*(enter MENELAUS wearing crown)*

**MENELAUS:** I am the King of Sparta!

**CHORUS 2:** He also got to marry the king's other daughter, Helen, who is the most beautiful woman in the world.

*(enter HELEN)*

**HELEN:** I am. Let's go dear.

*(MENELAUS and HELEN exit holding hands)*

**CHORUS 3:** Agamemnon returned from Sparta, killed his uncle, and reclaimed the throne!

**CHORUS 1:** Oh, just like Hamlet!

**CHORUS 2:** No, like Lion King.

**CHORUS 3:** Would you two stop. Those stories were based on this story!

**CHORUS 1&2:** Cool!

**CHORUS 3:** So that's kind of how this current war got started. You see, a few years later, King Paris of Troy stopped in for a not-so-friendly visit.

*(HELEN enters; PARIS enters opposite)*

**PARIS:** You are the one Aphrodite promised me.

**HELEN:** I am?

**PARIS:** You shall come with me.

**HELEN:** I will?

*(PARIS takes HELEN by the wrist and leads her offstage)*

**HELEN:** HELP!!! Stranger danger!!!

**CHORUS 1:** They returned to Troy. Menelaus and his brother Agamemnon, Atreus' sons in vengeful ire, 'gainst Paris, started a war to get her back.

*(enter AGAMEMNON and MENELAUS)*

**AGAMEMNON:** Let's get your wife back!

**AGAMEMNON & MENELAUS:** Charge! *(both exit)*

**CHORUS 2:** But, a terrible price had to be paid at the start of this war. King Agamemnon made a fatal error.

**CHORUS 3:** He insulted the goddess Artemis, by boasting he was a better hunter than her. What hubris!

**CHORUS 1:** Bad idea. I've met Artemis. She's not just the goddess of the hunt, she's a friggin' furious warrior!

*(enter ARTEMIS flanked by huntresses)*

**ARTEMIS:** How dare this pesky mortal insult me! ME! Such arrogance! *(big, magical gesture)*

**CHORUS 2:** Artemis stopped the winds so he could not sail. The only way to recover was to sacrifice his daughter, Iphigenia. His child to slay and with her spilt blood make an offering to Artemis.

*(scream heard backstage)*

**CHORUS 3:** Dark.

**ARTEMIS:** Oooh... dark... You got a problem with that? *(CHORUS shakes heads)* Good. Ladies, let's ride! *(exits with huntresses)*

**CHORUS 1:** The queen was sooo mad at him!

**CLYTEMNESTRA:** *(enters with servants)* Nothing worse than a woman scorned!

**CHORUS 2:** *(whispers)* So mad she got a boyfriend while he was gone. Together, they plotted to kill Agamemnon upon his return. Speaking of...

**CHORUS 3:** Queen Clytemnestra, speak and say what messenger of joy today? Is there news of the war?

**CLYTEMNESTRA:** Troy is ours! The war is won!

*(CHORUS cheers; TOWNSPEOPLE enter; enter HERALD)*

**HERALD:** O land of Argos, fatherland of mine! After ten long years the war has ended and we have returned home!

**CHORUS 1:** Herald! How was the war?

**HERALD:** We sailed through terrible storms. Slept in the dirt. Ate worms. It was miserable FOR TEN YEARS! But, it's over now.

**CHORUS 2:** Worms, seriously?

**HERALD:** Frog legs, too. Tastes like chicken! Look, out of darkness dawns a light. Agamemnon has returned!

*(enter AGAMEMNON, CASSANDRA, and SOLDIERS; ALL bow)*

**AGAMEMNON:** What a war! We have made them pay for stealing Helen. Now to my palace and the shrines of home.

**CLYTEMNESTRA:** Oh, citizens of Argos! I will speak my love for my husband!

**CHORUS 3:** This should be good.

**CLYTEMNESTRA:** Ten long years I have waited! I sent our children away for their safety, which left me all alone to cry. ALL. ALONE. For me, long since the gushing fount of tears is swept away; no drop is left to shed.

**AGAMEMNON:** Sheesh, I get it. But, I was at war, not off playing video games! Again.

**CLYTEMNESTRA:** Whatever. Welcome home, husband! Servants, lay down the cloths so that my husband may walk upon them.

*(SERVANTS lay down purple cloth)*

**AGAMEMNON:** I don't think I should. A mortal man to set foot on those rich dyes? Sounds like hubris to me and we all know how that turned out last time.

**CLYTEMNESTRA:** Argos has tons of purple cloth lying around. Walk on the cloth, it's ok.

**AGAMEMNON:** Nah, I'm good.

**CLYTEMNESTRA:** I bet the other kings are walking on cloths right now. Are you not as great as they are?

**AGAMEMNON:** Ok, ok, sheesh! I'll walk on the cloths. *(walks on cloth)* By the way, this is Cassandra, princess of Troy. She is the prize and flower of all we won.

**CLYTEMNESTRA:** She's your... flower?

**AGAMEMNON:** My reward. Elders, take care of her, I'm off to my palace. *(AGAMEMNON exits with SOLDIERS)*

**CLYTEMNESTRA:** Zeus, let me have my revenge! *(looks upward)* LIKE NOW!!!

**CHORUS 1:** I've got a bad feeling about this.

**CHORUS 2:** Wow! Look at her evil glare!

**CHORUS 3:** Wicked!

**CLYTEMNESTRA:** Hey, Cassandra! *(pause)* Do you hear me?

*(CASSANDRA stares off)*

**CLYTEMNESTRA**: Yo, flower girl. Get inside! *(to audience)* She had better stay out of my way. No one ever accused me of having a green thumb, if you know what I mean. *(evil laugh)*

*(CASSANDRA still staring)*

**CLYTEMNESTRA**: *(to CHORUS)* Does she understand me? Helloooooo!

**CHORUS 1**: *(to CASSANDRA)* You should probably listen to her.

*(CASSANDRA continues staring)*

**CLYTEMNESTRA**: I don't have time for this! The Elders can deal with you. *(ALL exit, except CHORUS and CASSANDRA)*

**CHORUS 2**: Come, poor child.

**CASSANDRA**: Apollo! God of all ways, but only Death's to me.

**CHORUS 3**: She speaks! But I have no idea what she says. *(CHORUS shrugs)*

**CASSANDRA**: Apollo, your curse has led me from one horror to another! You gave me the gift of seeing, but not being believed.

**CHORUS 1**: *(aside to other CHORUS)* Maybe she's mad.

**CHORUS 2**: She says she is a prophet! Maybe she knows something we don't. *(to CASSANDRA)* Do you know where you are? You're at Agamemnon's palace.

**CASSANDRA**: *(frantic)* No! This is a house of despair! It is cursed! *(has a vision)* A bath, a trap! She smites him!

**CHORUS 3**: Yep! She's mad.

**CASSANDRA:** The King will be killed! I will also die! But an avenger will come!

**CHORUS 2:** Iron Man? *(CHORUS glares)* What? I'm a big fan.

**CASSANDRA:** I was right about the fall of Troy and I'm right about this. No one ever believes me. *(cries)*

**CHORUS 1:** There, there. We believe you, don't we?

*(CHORUS mumbles and shrugs, looks at her like she's crazy)*

**CASSANDRA:** I wish Apollo never gave me this "gift." *(exits crying)*

**AGAMEMNON:** *(screams from offstage)* I am murdered! *(CHORUS gasp; AGAMEMNON runs onstage)* Murdered! Oh, they got me while I was in the bath! Not cool! Isn't anyone coming to save me? *(CLYTEMNESTRA enters, pulls AGAMEMNON offstage while screaming)* O I am sped - a deep, a moral blow!

**CHORUS 3:** I think the king has been killed!

**CHORUS 1:** Ya think??

**CHORUS 2:** What should we do?

**CHORUS 3:** Sit back and watch, this is entertaining! *(nods for audience's agreement)*

**CLYTEMNESTRA:** *(enters triumphantly)* Finally, vengeance for my murdered child, Iphigenia.

**CHORUS 1:** Bless you.

**CLYTEMNESTRA**: And I had help from my secret boyfriend, Aegisthus. Isn't that right, honey?

**AEGISTHUS**: *(enters)* That's right! I am Agamemnon's cousin and I also wanted him dead! His dad killed my brothers and secretly served them to my father for dinner!

**CHORUS 2**: Gross!

**CHORUS 3**: It's Titus Andronicus! You sure Shakespeare didn't write this?

**CHORUS 1**: I'm gonna be sick. *(retching, runs off stage)*

**AEGISTHUS**: Dawn of the day of rightful vengeance!

**CLYTEMNESTRA**: I also got rid of that annoying Cassandra. No one ignores me, flower or not!

**CASSANDRA**: *(enters)* Wait, I'm dead already? The play just started.

**CLYTEMNESTRA**: I suppose you should have SEEN it coming. Bye, bye, Petunia.

*(CASSANDRA falls over dead)*

**CLYTEMNESTRA**: *(to AEGISTHUS)* I and thou will rule the palace. *(exits with AEGISTHUS)*

*(CHORUS 1 returns)*

**CHORUS 2**: Wow. Cassandra was right.

**CASSANDRA**: FINALLY! Someone believes me! *(dies again)*

**CHORUS 3:** This sure is one crazy family!

**CHORUS 1:** But, remember, she said there would be an avenger?

**CHORUS 2:** Thor, right? He's an avenger AND a god.

*(CHORUS glares again)*

**CHORUS 3:** I bet Agamemnon's son will return and avenge his father's death!

**CHORUS 1:** Oh, yeah! Orestes, I forgot about him!

**CHORUS 2:** Well, this whole trilogy is kind of named after him.

*(CHORUS mumbles in agreement)*

*(ALL exit)*

## Act Two - The Libation Bearers

Outside Argos, the tomb of Agamemnon

*(Someone walks by with a sign that says, "PLAY 2 - The Libation Bearers. Several years later"; enter ORESTES)*

**ORESTES:** After all these years, me, who from banishment returning, stand on this, my country and my father's grave.

*(enter ELECTRA carrying libations and followed by CHORUS)*

**ORESTES:** I see Electra, mine own sister with her servants approaching my father's grave! I wonder what they are doing?

*(ORESTES hides and watches)*

**CHORUS 4:** *(to audience)* We have been sent by Clytemnestra to bring libations for the dead.

**CHORUS 5:** She's trying to make up for the fact that she murdered her husband!

**CHORUS 6:** *(motions to ELECTRA)* HER dad.

**CHORUS 4:** Awkward!

**ELECTRA:** *(to CHORUS)* This offering is a tribute to my father. But, it comes from his killer, my mother. Please, counsel me!

**CHORUS 6:** Pray for Orestes to return and avenge your father's death.

**ELECTRA:** Great idea! *(speaks to gods)* I ask for Orestes, who shall the slayer slay. There, that should do it!

*(ORESTES comes out of hiding)*

**ORESTES:** I am he, Orestes, and I have come to avenge my father!

**CHORUS 5:** Wow, that was fast! *(to audience)* He's no Thor, though.

**ELECTRA:** How did you know to come?

**ORESTES:** The oracle of Apollo told me I must come and avenge my father, or the Gods would punish me with horrible diseases, wreaking their wrath on me.

**CHORUS 4:** Yuck!

**ELECTRA:** Well, last night, mom had a terror of a dream that she gave birth to a snake, and it bit her. She totally freaked, then sent us to offer libations so the gods don't punish her.

**ORESTES:** This dream - it bodes a man's revenge! I am that snake!

**CHORUS 5:** Okaaaaay. Weirdo.

**ORESTES:** Just, go inside and act normal.

*(ELECTRA and CHORUS nod and exit; ORESTES knocks on door)*

**ORESTES:** Hello? Anyone home?

**CLYTEMNESTRA:** *(entering)* Oh, I hope it's not Artemis trying to get me to join her hunters again. Oh good, it's just some random guy. *(to ORESTES)* What do you want, stranger?

**ORESTES:** Stranger? Yes! I am a stranger, with a message for you. Your son, Orestes, is no more. Sorry. Dead. Bummer.

**CLYTEMNESTRA:** No! That can't be! You had better come in.

*(CLYTEMNESTRA and ORESTES exit; CHORUS enters)*

**CHORUS 6**: I hope Orestes knows what he's doing.

**CHORUS 4**: Look, here comes Orestes' nurse.

**CHORUS 5**: It looks like she's crying.

**NURSE**: The Queen ordered me to get Aegisthus so that he can hear the news himself.

**CHORUS 6**: Is the queen upset?

**NURSE**: She is pretending to be sad… but I know she is happy her son is dead.

**CHORUS 4**: *(shaking her head)* His own mother!

**CHORUS 5**: With no male heir of Agamemnon left, they remain on the throne.

**NURSE**: But I truly am sad. I cared for Orestes since birth, and now he's dead. Well, I guess I'll go fetch Aegisthus.

**CHORUS 6**: Wait, are you to tell Aegisthus to bring henchmen or to come alone?

**NURSE**: The queen bids him bring a spear-armed bodyguard.

**CHORUS 4**: Maybe, leave that part out.

**NURSE**: *(shrugs)* OK. *(exits)*

**CHORUS 5**: Orestes will now have a chance for his revenge. Look, here comes Aegisthus.

**AEGISTHUS**: *(enters)* I heard a traveler arrived with a new rumor. Orestes is dead?

**CHORUS 6**: *(shrugs)* Dunno. Why don't you go inside and find out?

**AEGISTHUS**: I shall! *(exits; pause; screams)* Help, help, alas!

**NURSE:** *(runs onstage)* Someone has killed Aegisthus! *(dramatically)* My lord is done to death! *(calmly)* See, I can pretend to be upset, too.

*(CHORUS applaud, NURSE curtsies)*

**CLYTEMNESTRA:** *(enters)* What's with all the shouting?

**NURSE:** My Queen, Aegisthus has been killed.

**CLYTEMNESTRA:** What?!? No!

*(NURSE exits; ORESTES enters with AEGISTHUS who shrugs and dies)*

**CLYTEMNESTRA:** *(sobbing)* No, not my love!

**ORESTES:** What, lov'st the man? Then in his grave lie down.

**CLYTEMNESTRA:** Well... I may not have loved him THAT much... Wait! It's YOU! Take pity on your mother! I gave birth to you!

**ORESTES:** Hmmm, that is true. *(to CHORUS)* What should I do? I'm confused! Should I spare my mother?

**CHORUS 4:** Well, Apollo did foretell this at Delphi. You probably don't want to make him mad. Being a god and all.

**ORESTES:** Soooo, choose between my mom or a god that will strike me down with a horrendous disease?

**CHORUS 5:** Right!

**ORESTES:** Ok, then. *(leads Clytemnestra to Aegisthus)* You chose him over my father, I will slay thee at his side.

**CLYTEMNESTRA**: WHAT?! Ummm... your father did sacrifice your sister, remember?

**ORESTES**: He was fighting in a war while you plotted his death with another man!

**CLYTEMNESTRA**: Well, he was gone an awfully long time. 'Tis hard for wives to live as widows, child.

**ORESTES**: No excuses! I am the snake in your dream!

**CHORUS 4**: Wow, he's really gonna do it.

**CHORUS 5**: That's got to be bad karma.

**CHORUS 6**: Maybe now this land can know peace... or probably just more murdering.

*(ORESTES kills CLYTEMNESTRA)*

**ORESTES**: Here are the tyrants who killed my father and stole the crown. I say that rightfully I slew my mother. *(sounding a bit crazy)* The gods would never punish me for this, right?

**CHORUS 4**: I think he's losing it.

**ORESTES**: *(crazier)* They were bad people! Apollo told me to do it!

**CHORUS 5**: Yep, insane in the membrane.

**ORESTES**: *(and crazier)* I must away!

**CHORUS 6**: Good idea. Go on a nice little trip... away from here.

**ORESTES**: Do you guys see those ghosts? *(pointing offstage)*

**CHORUS 4**: He's loony.

**CHORUS 5**: Go to Apollo! *(shoves ORESTES offstage)*

**CHORUS 6**: That guy needs some serious therapy.

**CHORUS 4**: Wait, the play doesn't end like this, does it? This is a mess!

**CHORUS 5**: Remember, this is a trilogy. There's one more play left.

**CHORUS 6**: Oh yeah! Thank the gods.

**CHORUS 4**: It must have all the happy stuff in it. I'm sure everything will turn out juuuust fine. *(CHORUS 5 & 6 pats CHORUS 4 on the back as ALL exit)*

## Act Three - The Eumenides

*(someone walks by with a sign that says, "Play 3 - The Eumenides - Several days later"; CHORUS and ORESTES enter; CHORUS chanting, surround ORESTES; APOLLO enters)*

**APOLLO:** SLEEP! *(CHORUS and ORESTES sleep)* Whew, I'm glad those furies are quiet. They better not wake up. Nothing like the goddesses of vengeance to ruin your day. *(notices audience)* Oh! Well, hello! Welcome to Delphi and the temple of... me! You know, Apollo. The coolest god around. Anyway, time to help my little buddy here. *(whispering)* Orestes!

**ORESTES:** *(sadly)* What?

**APOLLO:** I know for by my hest thou didst thy mother slay. But, wow, I didn't think you'd actually do it! That was entertaining!

**ORESTES:** Entertaining? *(to the audience)* Talk about mixed messages.

**APOLLO:** Listen, go to Athens and the goddess Athena will give you a trial. I'll put in a good word for you. She's my half sister, and she loves me. Well, everybody loves me. I got your back, bro.

**ORESTES:** Yeah, ok. If you say so... bro. *(exits, APOLLO exits opposite)*

**CLYTEMNESTRA:** *(enters)* The wandering ghost that once was Clytemnestra calls - Arise! *(CHORUS doesn't move)* My own son killed me! ARISE!!! *(CHORUS rises)* While you furies were sleeping, he got away! Go after him!

*(CHORUS standing and ready to fight; CLYTEMNESTRA exits; APOLLO enters)*

**APOLLO:** Are you gals still here? Out! I command you!

**CHORUS 7**: This is all your fault. Thine oracle bade this man slay his mother.

**CHORUS 8**: Not cool!

**APOLLO**: Chill out. I simply said to avenge a wife who slays her lord.

**CHORUS 9**: He came back here for your protection!

**CHORUS 7**: We followed him all the way here, and there are no planes in Ancient Greece. We had to walk! I loathe walking!

**APOLLO**: Waah! Why were you bothering Orestes, but not Clytemnestra? She killed her husband!

**CHORUS 8**: He wasn't her blood. Plus Agamemnon was kind of a meanie.

**CHORUS 9**: We will haunt Orestes forever for killing his mom.

**APOLLO**: *(mocking CHORUS)* We will haunt Orestes forever... Whatever. If you want him so badly, follow then!! But, I do like him, so I will save him. Oh, and guess what? I CAN fly. Smell ya later! *(APOLLO exits with a flurry)*

**CHORUS 8**: Ohhh... I REALLY don't like that guy!!!

**CHORUS 7**: We have to walk again?! Ugh...

*(CHORUS exits; someone walks by with a sign that says, "Outside the temple of Athena in Athens")*

**ORESTES**: *(enters and kneels)* I call Athena, lady of this land. Apollo told me I should come stand trial. Please be merciful.

*(CHORUS enters)*

**CHORUS 9**: There he is.

**CHORUS 7**: Finally! My feet are killing me!

**CHORUS 8**: I'm so sick of chasing him around!

**ORESTES**: Oh no, you gals again? Look, I'm pretty sure Athena will take pity on me and Apollo is totally on my side.

**CHORUS 9**: Thee, not Apollo nor Athena's strength, can save from perishing.

**CHORUS 7**: Don't make him run again! I'm tired!

**CHORUS 8**: I've got an idea! Let's cast a binding spell so he can't move!

**CHORUS 9**: We can do that?

**CHORUS 7**: Ah, yeah. We're furies. We rock.

*(CHORUS does a wild magical gesture toward ORESTES, who freezes in place; CHORUS high fives; ATHENA enters)*

**ATHENA**: What mischief abounds? Who are ye?

**CHORUS 8**: Goddess Athena! We are the children of eternal night, and furies in the underworld. We've been haunting this dude for pages now.

**ATHENA**: Oh, the vengeance ladies. What hath this insignificant mortal done?

**CHORUS 9**: He did his mother slay.

**ATHENA**: Hmmm... I suppose that could be bad. But, why?

**CHORUS 7:** She did kill his dad.

*(CHORUS 8 & 9 shush her)*

**ATHENA:** A conundrum! Too mighty is this matter. I know! We shall have a trial! I, of course, shall be judge, because, well, I AM the goddess of wisdom. And we will have a jury of Athenians. *(exits)*

**CHORUS 8:** Seriously, a trial? Boring!

**CHORUS 9:** Let's rip him to pieces.

**CHORUS 7:** I like how you think.

*(CHORUS creeps toward ORESTES; ATHENA enters with JURY; CHORUS acts innocent, unfreezes ORESTES)*

**ATHENA:** Let the trial begin. Jury, stand over there.

*(EVERYONE takes their "court" positions; APOLLO enters)*

**CHORUS 8:** Apollo, why are you here?

**APOLLO:** I came to defend Orestes.

**CHORUS 9:** You're not a lawyer!

**APOLLO:** I'm a god!

**CHORUS 7:** That does sound like a lawyer.

**ATHENA:** Hello, brother.

**APOLLO:** Yo! What up, Thena!

**ATHENA:** Alright! Let's begin. Tell the tale first and set the matter clear.

**CHORUS 8:** Orestes, hast then thy mother slain??

**ORESTES:** I slew her. I deny no word hereof.

**CHORUS 9:** We rest our case.

**CHORUS 7:** Off with his head!

**ORESTES:** Wait! I killed her, but Apollo told me to. Plus, she killed my father.

**CHORUS 8:** But, she was not kin by blood to him she slew.

**CHORUS 9:** Yeah, it's way worse to kill someone of your own blood.

**CHORUS 7:** Off with his head!

**APOLLO:** *(to ORESTES)* I got this, bro. *(to the JURY)* She was only his mom. The male is the parent! She was just a... a woman.

*(EVERYONE gasps)*

**CHORUS 8:** Hold me back! *(CHORUS 7 & 9 holds her back)*

**ORESTES:** *(to APOLLO)* Dude, I'm not sure that's the best defense.

**APOLLO:** Shhh... That he should die, a chieftain, and a king... by female hands! Shameful.

**ATHENA:** Ok, enough is said. Furies, do you rest your case?

**CHORUS:** Yes.

**ATHENA:** Apollo, do you rest your case?

**APOLLO:** *(looking at himself in a mirror)* What? Yeah, sure.

**ATHENA**: Jurors, make your decision.

*(JURY huddles)*

**ATHENA**: *(to audience)* Citizens of Athens, we had our first trial! Well, go ahead, applaud for me. *(coax audience to applaud)* Wow, I'm super smart! How's it going jury?

**JUROR**: It's a tie. We cannot agree.

**ATHENA**: Hmmm, well mine is the right to add the final vote. I say Orestes will go free! I like him. He's cute.

*(CHORUS pouts; ORESTES and APOLLO high five; JURY exits)*

**APOLLO**: I'm good at this lawyering stuff.

**ORESTES**: Wow! I was pretty sure those furies were going to rip me to pieces.

**CHORUS**: We still can!

**ORESTES**: Ok, then... I will return to rule Argos. And now farewell thou and thy city's folk. And especially you monsters! *(points to CHORUS)*

*(APOLLO and ORESTES exit)*

**CHORUS 9**: Well that stinks. We didn't even get to rip anyone to pieces.

**CHORUS 7**: What are we going to do now?

**CHORUS 8**: I don't want to go anywhere near Apollo, that's for sure. That guy's a pig!

**ATHENA**: Ladies, be appeased. You mighty deities shall stay in Athens. You can help good people and punish the bad. Instead of just punishing all the time.

**CHORUS 9**: That doesn't sound too bad.

**CHORUS 7**: Yeah, and no more walking!

**ATHENA**: You will be known as The Eumenides.

**CHORUS 8**: The what now?

**ATHENA**: The Eumenides. It means "the kindly ones".

**CHORUS 9**: That's what that means!

**CHORUS 7**: I've been wondering this whole time.

**CHORUS 8**: *(to the audience)* Alright people, who's been good...

**CHORUS**: And who's been naughty?

*(CHORUS run offstage; ATHENA follows shaking her head)*

### THE END

**Pronunciations:**

Clytemnestra: cly-tehm-nes-truh
Agamemnon: ag-a-mehm-non
Atreus: ay-tree-uhs
Menalaus: meh-nuh-lay-uhs
Artemis: aar-tuh-muhs
Aegisthus: ee-jis-thus
Orestes: aw-reh-stees
Electra: e-lec-trah
Iphigenia: if-uh-juh-nee-uh
Eumenides: yoo-meh-nuh-deez

## Author's note and Special Thanks

Growing up Greek plays were exactly that, Greek to me. I didn't understand them and surely was not engaged by them. Fast forward 40 years and I ask myself, "What was I thinking?!" Because Greek plays are a BLAST! Treachery, tragedy, gods, human emotions, AND the basis of so many stories we know today.

After multiple requests from teachers, I finally did it and completed my first Greek play. A big THANK YOU to all those teachers who pushed me. Trust me when I say, this was the first, and WILL NOT be the last!

First, a big shout out to Mr. Murray's Theatre Class at Crespo Elementary in the Houston Independent School District. He workshopped this play with his classes. I always love the creative ideas the kids bring!

And as always, a big thank you to all my beta readers who are ALWAYS improving my scripts! Isidro (very snarky, sir!), David, Bridget, Royce, and Laura. What a great list! My books are not what their potential is, without the Betas!!!

-Brendan

## Sneak Peeks at other Playing With Plays books:

| | |
|---|---|
| Tempest for Kids | Pg 77 |
| Two Gentlemen of Verona for Kids | Pg 79 |
| A Christmas Carol for Kids | Pg 82 |
| Oliver Twist for Kids | Pg 85 |
| Macbeth for Kids | Pg 87 |
| Beowulf for Kids | Pg 89 |
| Jekyll & Hyde for Kids | Pg 91 |
| The Legend of Sleepy Hollow for Kids | Pg 94 |
| Hound of the Baskervilles for Kids | Pg 97 |

Sneak peek of
# The Tempest for Kids

**PROSPERO:** Hast thou, spirit, performed to point the tempest that I bade thee?

**ARIEL:** What? Was that English?

**PROSPERO:** *(Frustrated)* Did you make the storm hit the ship?

**ARIEL:** Why didn't you say that in the first place? Oh yeah! I rocked that ship! They didn't know what hit them.

**PROSPERO:** Why, that's my spirit! But are they, Ariel, safe?

**ARIEL:** Not a hair perished.

**PROSPERO:** Woo-hoo! All right. We've got more work to do.

**ARIEL:** Wait a minute. You're still going to free me, right, Master?

**PROSPERO:** Oh, I see. Is it sooooo terrible working for me? Huh? Remember when I saved you from that witch? Do you? Remember when that blue-eyed hag locked you up and left you for dead? Who saved you? Me, that's who!

**ARIEL:** I thank thee, master.

**PROSPERO:** I will free you in two days, okay? Sheesh. Patience is a virtue, or haven't you heard. Right. Where was I? Oh yeah... I need you to disguise yourself like a sea nymph and then... *(PROSPERO whispers something in ARIEL'S ear)* Got it?

**ARIEL:** Got it. *(ARIEL exits)*

**PROSPERO:** *(to MIRANDA)* Awake, dear heart, awake!

*(MIRANDA yawns loudly)*

**PROSPERO:** Shake it off. Come on. We'll visit Caliban, my slave.

**MIRANDA:** The witch's son? You mean the MONSTER! He's creepy and stinky!!!

**PROSPERO:** Mysterious and sneaky,

**MIRANDA:** Altogether freaky,

**MIRANDA & PROSPERO:** He's Caliban the slave!!! *(snap, snap!)*

**PROSPERO:** *(Calls offstage)* What, ho! Slave! Caliban!

*(enter CALIBAN)*

**CALIBAN:** Oh, look it's the island stealers! This is my home! My mother, the witch, left it to me and now you treat me like dirt.

**MIRANDA:** Oh boo-hoo! I used to feel sorry for you, I even taught you our language, but you tried to hurt me so now we have to lock you in that cave.

**CALIBAN:** I wish I had never learned your language!

**PROSPERO:** Go get us wood! If you don't, I'll rack thee with old cramps, and fill all thy bones with aches!

**CALIBAN:** *(to AUDIENCE)* He's so mean to me! But I have to do what he says. ANNOYING! *(exit CALIBAN)*

*(enter FERDINAND led by "invisible" ARIEL)*

**ARIEL:** *(Singing)* Who let the dogs out?! Woof, woof, woof!! *(Spookily)* The watchdogs bark; bow-wow, bow-wow!

**FERDINAND:** *(Dancing across stage)* Where should this music be? Where is it taking me! What's going on?

## Sneak peek of
# Two Gentlemen of Verona for Kids

**ANTONIO:** It's not nothing.

**PROTEUS:** Ahhhhh.......It's a letter from Valentine, telling me what a great time he's having in Milan, yeah... that's what it says!

**ANTONIO:** Awesome! Glad to hear it! Because, you leave tomorrow to join Valentine in Milan.

**PROTEUS:** What!? Dad! No way! I don't want... I mean, I need some time. I've got some things to do.

**ANTONIO:** Like what?

**PROTEUS:** You know...things! Important things! And stuff! Lots of stuff!

**ANTONIO:** No more excuses! Go pack your bag. *(ANTONIO begins to exit)*

**PROTEUS:** Fie!

**ANTONIO:** What was that?

**PROTEUS:** Fiiii......ne with me, Pops! *(ANTONIO exits)* I was afraid to show my father Julia's letter, lest he should take exceptions to my love; and my own lie of an excuse made it easier for him to send me away.

**ANTONIO:** *(Offstage)* Proteus! Get a move on!!

**PROTEUS:** Fie!!!

*(exit)*

### ACT 2 SCENE 1

*(enter VALENTINE and SPEED following)*

**VALENTINE:** Ah, Silvia, Silvia! *(heavy sighs)*

**SPEED**: *(mocking)* Madam Silvia! Madam Silvia! Gag me.

**VALENTINE**: Knock it off! You don't know her.

**SPEED**: Do too. She's the one that you can't stop staring at. Makes me wanna barf.

**VALENTINE**: I do not stare!

**SPEED**: You do. AND you keep singing that silly love song. *(sing INSERT SAPPY LOVE SONG)* You used to be so much fun.

**VALENTINE**: Huh? *(heavy sigh, starts humming SAME LOVE SONG)*

**SPEED**: Never mind.

**VALENTINE**: I have loved her ever since I saw her. Here she comes!

**SPEED**: Great. *(to audience)* Watch him turn into a fool.

*(enter SILVIA)*

**VALENTINE**: Hey, Silvia.

**SILVIA**: Hey, Valentine. What's goin' on?

**VALENTINE**: Nothin'. What's goin' on with you?

**SILVIA**: Nothin'.

*(pause)*

**VALENTINE**: What are you doing later?

**SILVIA**: Not sure. Prob-ly nothin'. You?

**VALENTINE**: Me neither. Nothin'.

**SILVIA**: Yea?

**VALENTINE**: Probably.

**SPEED:** *(to audience)* Kill me now.

**SILVIA:** Well, I guess I better go.

**VALENTINE:** Oh, okay! See ya'..

*(pause)*

**SILVIA:** See ya' later maybe?

**VALENTINE:** Oh, yea! Maybe! Yea! Okay!

**SILVIA:** Bye.

**VALENTINE:** Bye!

*(exit SILVIA)*

**SPEED:** *(aside)* Wow. *(to VALENTINE)* Dude, what the heck was that?

**VALENTINE:** I think she has a boyfriend. I can tell.

**SPEED:** Dude! She is so into you! How could you not see that?

**VALENTINE:** Do you think?

**SPEED:** Come on. We'll talk it through over dinner. *(to audience)* Fool. Am I right?

*(exit)*

Sneak peek of
# Christmas Carol for Kids

*(enter GHOST PRESENT wearing a robe and holding a turkey leg and a goblet)*

**GHOST PRESENT:** Wake up, Scrooge! I am the Ghost of Christmas Present. Look upon me!

**SCROOGE:** I'm looking. Not that impressed. But let's get on with it.

**GHOST PRESENT:** Touch my robe! *(SCROOGE touches GHOST PRESENT's robe. Pause. They look at each other)* Er...it must be broken. Guess we walk. Come on. *(they begin walking downstage)*

**SCROOGE:** Where are we going?

**GHOST PRESENT:** Your employee, Bob Cratchit's house. Oh look, here we are.

*(enter BOB, MRS. CRATCHIT, MARTHA CRATCHIT, and TINY TIM, who has a crutch in one hand; they are all holding bowls)*

**BOB:** *(to audience)* Hi, we're the Cratchit family. We are a REALLY happy family!

**MRS. CRATCHIT:** *(to audience)* Yes, but we're REALLY poor, too. Thanks to HIS boss! *(pointing at BOB)*

**MARTHA:** *(to audience)* Yeah, as you can see our bowls are empty. *(shows empty bowl)* We practically survive off air.

**TINY TIM:** *(to audience)* But we're happy!

**MRS. CRATCHIT:** *(to audience; overly sappy)* Because we have each other.

**TINY TIM:** And love!

**SCROOGE:** *(to GHOST PRESENT)* Seriously, are they for real?

**GHOST PRESENT:** Yep! Adorable, isn't it?

**BOB:** A merry Christmas to us all.

**TINY TIM:** God bless us every one!

**SCROOGE:** Spirit, tell me if Tiny Tim will live.

**GHOST PRESENT:** *(puts hands to head as if looking into the future)* Ooooo, not so good....I see a vacant seat in the poor chimney corner, and a crutch without an owner. If SOMEBODY doesn't change SOMETHING, the child will die.

**SCROOGE:** No, no! Say he will be spared.

**GHOST PRESENT:** Nope, can't do that, sorry. Unless SOMEONE decides to change...hint, hint.

**BOB:** A Christmas toast to my boss, Mr. Scrooge! The founder of the feast!

**MRS. CRATCHIT:** *(angrily)* Oh sure, Mr. Scrooge! If he were here I'd give him a piece of my mind to feast upon. What an odious, stingy, hard, unfeeling man!

**BOB:** Dear, it's Christmas day. He's not THAT bad. *(Pause)* He's just... THAT sad. *(BOB holds up his bowl)* Come on, kids, to Scrooge! He probably needs it more than us!

**MARTHA & TINY TIM:** *(holding up their bowls)* To Scrooge!

**MRS. CRATCHIT:** *(muttering)* Thanks for nothing.

**BOB:** That's not nice.

**MARTHA:** And we Cratchits are ALWAYS nice. Read

the book, Mom.

**MRS. CRATCHIT:** Sorry.

*(the CRATCHIT FAMILY exits)*

**SCROOGE:** She called me odious! Do I really smell that bad?

**GHOST PRESENT:** Odious doesn't mean you stink. Although in this case you do… According to the dictionary, odious means "unequivocally detestable." I mean, you are a toad sometimes Mr. Scrooge.

**SCROOGE:** Wow… that's kind of … mean.

Sneak peek of
# Oliver Twist for Kids

*(enter FAGIN, SIKES, DODGER and NANCY)*

**DODGER**: So that Oliver kid got caught by the police.

**FAGIN**: He could tell them all our secrets and get us in trouble; we've got to find him. Like, in the next 30 seconds or so.

**SIKES**: Send Nancy. She's good at getting information quick.

**NANCY**: Nope. Don't wanna go, Sikes. I like the kid.

**SIKES**: She'll go, Fagin.

**NANCY**: No, she won't, Fagin.

**SIKES**: Yes, she will, Fagin.

**NANCY**: Fine! Grrrrr….

*(NANCY sticks out her tongue at SIKES and storms offstage, then immediately returns)*

**NANCY**: Okay, I checked with my sources and, some gentleman took him home to take care of him.

*(NANCY, DODGER and SIKES stare at FAGIN waiting for direction)*

**FAGIN**: Where?

**NANCY**: I don't know.

**FAGIN:** WHAT!?!? *(waiting)* Well don't just stand there, GO FIND HIM! *(to audience)* Can't find any good help these days!

*(all run offstage, bumping into each other in their haste)*

## ACT 2 SCENE 2

*(enter OLIVER)*

**OLIVER:** *(to audience)* I'm out running an errand for Mr. Brownlow to prove that I'm a trustworthy boy. I can't keep hanging out with thieves, right?

*(enter NANCY, who runs over to OLIVER and grabs him; SIKES, FAGIN, and DODGER enter shortly after and follow NANCY)*

**NANCY:** Oh my dear brother! I've found him! Oh! Oliver! Oliver!

**OLIVER:** What!?!? I don't have a sister!

**NANCY:** You do now, kid. Let's go. *(she drags OLIVER to FAGIN)*

**FAGIN:** Dodger, take Oliver and lock him up.

**DODGER:** *(to OLIVER)* Sorry, dude. *(DODGER and OLIVER start to exit)*

**OLIVER:** Aw, man! Seriously? I just found a good home...

**NANCY:** Don't be too mean to him, Fagin.

**OLIVER:** *(as he's exiting)* Yeah, don't be too mean to me, Fagin!

**SIKES:** *(mimicking NANCY)* Don't be mean, Fagin. Wah, wah, wah. Look, I need Oliver to help me rob a house, okay? He is just the size I want to fit through the window. All sneaky ninja like.

Sneak peek of
# Macbeth for Kids
## ACT 2 SCENE 1

*(DUNCAN runs on stage and dies with a dagger stuck in him, MACBETH drags his body off and then returns with the bloody dagger. LADY MACBETH enters)*

**LADY MACBETH:** Did you do it?

**MACBETH:** *(clueless)* Do what?

**LADY MACBETH:** KILL HIM!

**MACBETH:** Oh yeah, all done. I have done the deed.

**LADY MACBETH:** *(pointing at the dagger)* What is that?

**MACBETH:** What?

**LADY MACBETH:** Why do you still have the bloody dagger with you?

**MACBETH:** Ummmmm, I don't know.

**LADY MACBETH:** Well go put it back!

**MACBETH:** NO! I'll go no more! I'm scared of the dark, and there is a dead body in there. I am afraid to think what I have done.

**LADY MACBETH:** Man you are a wimp, give me the dagger. *(LADY MACBETH takes the dagger, exits, and returns)*

**LADY MACBETH:** All done.

*(there is a loud knock at the door)*

**LADY MACBETH:** It's 2am! This really is not a good time for more visitors. *(goes to the door)* Who is it? *(opens door)*

**MACDUFF**: It is Macduff. I am here to see the king.

**MACBETH**: He is sleeping in there.

*(MACDUFF exits while MACBETH and LADY MACBETH look at each other)*

**MACDUFF**: *(offstage scream)* AGHHHHHHHHHHH – He's dead, he's dead!!! *(MACDUFF enters)*

**MACBETH**: Who?

**MACDUFF**: Who do you think? *(they both scream)*

**BANQUO**: *(BANQUO, MALCOLM, and DONALBAIN enter)* What happened, can't someone get a good night sleep around here?

**MACDUFF**: The king has been murdered.

**MALCOLM & DONALBAIN**: Aghhhhhhhh!!!!!!!!!

**DONALBAIN**: We must be next.

**MALCOLM**: Let's get out of here.

**DONALBAIN**: I'm heading to Ireland.

**MALCOLM**: I'm off to England. *(MALCOLM and DONALBAIN exit)*

**MACDUFF**: Well, since there is no one left to be King, why don't you do it Mac?

**LADY MACBETH & MACBETH**: Okay. *(LADY MACBETH, MACBETH and MACDUFF exit)*

**BANQUO**: *(to audience)* I fear, thou play'dst most foully for't. *(MACBETH returns)*

**MACBETH**: Bank, what are you thinking over there?

**BANQUO**: Oh, nothing. *(said with a big fake smile)* Gotta go! See ya! *(BANQUO exits)*

# Sneak peek of
# Beowulf for Kids
## HROTHGAR and BEOWULF

*(enter HROTHGAR and DANES)*

**HROTHGAR:** *(wailing)* What have I done?! I have created a great hall and have put my people in danger! Hopefully, this monster will not come back again!

*(exit HROTHGAR; enter GRENDEL)*

**GRENDEL:** *(whistling; addresses audience)* Off to eat some more people! *(knocks at door, someone answers)* Rawwrr!!! I am the monster of evil, greedy and cruel, by the name of Grendel! Prepare to be eaten… again!

*(GRENDEL eats some more people, wipes his mouth with a napkin, and runs off stage; enter HROTHGAR)*

**HROTHGAR:** Noooooo! The monster has come back and will probably keep coming back for 12 years before someone comes to help us!

*(HROTHGAR and his DANES wail loudly; DANE 2 crosses the stage with a sign that says "12 Years Later"; enter BEOWULF and GEAT SOLDIERS)*

**BEOWULF:** I, the great and mighty Beowulf, warrior and champion of the Geats, servant to King Hygelac, have heard of your sorrows and have come to help!

*(ALL stop crying)*

**HROTHGAR:** How did you hear of our sorrows?

**BEOWULF:** *(leaning close to HROTHGAR, whispers)* Dude, you have been crying super loud for like 12 years, and I'm right offstage over there.

**HROTHGAR:** *(embarrassed, wipes face)* Oh right. *(cough)* Yes. Thank you for coming to our aid!

**BEOWULF:** I, the great Beowulf, alone now with Grendel I shall manage the matter, with the monster of evil.

**HROTHGAR:** Whew, that's a relief! I have been trying to figure out how to defeat Grendel for years and have failed. He's stopped by 4,380 times to feast on us!

**BEOWULF:** I never fail! I have defeated many a monster in my day! Including a sea monster... which is extra cool.

**UNFERTH:** Boooooo. That sea monster wasn't even that big!

**BEOWULF:** Who are you? And YES IT WAS!

**UNFERTH:** I am Unferth, great warrior for Hrothgar.

**BEOWULF:** *(to audience)* Obviously not THAT great. *(to UNFERTH)* You are just jealous of my greatness!

**UNFERTH:** Am not!

**BEOWULF:** Are too! And I heard you killed your brothers!

**UNFERTH:** Wow, that's a low blow... but... uhhhhh.... okay fine. I'll hang out right over here...

**HROTHGAR:** ANYWAY, back to me and MY problems.

**BEOWULF:** Right. Only with hand-grip the foe I must grapple, fight for my life then. If he win in the struggle, to eat in the war-hall earls of the geat-folk, boldly to swallow them.

**GEAT SOLDIER 1:** Wait... what was that?

**BEOWULF:** Sorry, quoting old text there.... I am going to fight Grendel with my bare hands. If I win, he dies. If I lose, he gets to eat all of us, including you!

Sneak peek of
# Jekyll and Hyde for Kids

**UTTERSON:** *(looks around)* Now, where is Hyde hiding?

**NARRATOR:** And they meet...

*(enter HYDE)*

**UTTERSON:** Mr. Hyde, I think?

**HYDE:** *(taken aback, and hisses)* That is my name. What's your issue?

**UTTERSON:** I am looking for Dr. Jekyll.

**HYDE:** He's not here.

**UTTERSON:** Let me see your face, sir.

**HYDE:** Why? Tell me how you know of me?

**UTTERSON:** We have common friends.

**HYDE:** *(snarls)* LIAR!!! *(suddenly exits)*

**UTTERSON:** Rude! *(to audience)* Did you see that murderous mixture of timidity and boldness? He seemed hardly human. I need to see Dr. Jekyll! *(walks across stage; knocks on door; POOLE enters)* Hello Poole, is Dr. Jekyll in?

**POOLE:** I'm sorry sir, but Dr. Jekyll is out.

**UTTERSON:** What can you tell me about Edward Hyde? I see he has a key to the back room.

**POOLE:** Ah, yes. Mr. Hyde has a key. We have orders to obey him.

**UTTERSON:** Thank you.

**POOLE:** Good day, sir. *(POOLE exits)*

**UTTERSON:** *(to audience)* That evil Hyde definitely has secrets of his own, black secrets. What has Jekyll gotten himself into?

*(UTTERSON exits)*

## ACT 1 SCENE 3

### Dr. Jekyll Was Quite at Ease

*(enter DR. JEKYLL, UTTERSON)*

**NARRATOR:** Soon, Dr. Jekyll hosted a party, and Utterson was determined to question his dear old friend...

**JEKYLL:** Thank you for coming to my pleasant dinner party. I always enjoy your company, Mr. Utterson.

**UTTERSON:** I've been wanting to speak to you, Jekyll. You know that will of yours?

**JEKYLL:** You are unfortunate in such a client. I never saw a man so distressed as you were by my will.

**UTTERSON:** You know I never approved of it.

**JEKYLL:** Yes, you have told me so.

**UTTERSON:** Well, I tell you again. Because I have learned more of young Hyde. What I heard was abominable.

**JEKYLL:** *(surprised)* Listen to me. DROP THIS. You do not understand my position.

**UTTERSON:** Jekyll, I am a man to be trusted. I am a lawyer. *(NARRATOR starts laughing; to NARRATOR)* Don't laugh.

**NARRATOR:** Sorry, you said "trust" and "lawyer" in the same sentence. And…yeah… My bad. Go on.

**UTTERSON:** *(to JEKYLL)* Tell me in confidence and I can get you out of it.

**JEKYLL:** I can be rid of Mr. Hyde when I choose. This is a private matter, and I beg of you to let it sleep.

**UTTERSON:** Fine, I will let it go… for now.

**JEKYLL:** Good.

# Sneak peek of
# The Legend of Sleepy Hollow for Kids

*(enter DIEDRICH, stands behind podium)*

**DIEDRICH:** This is a true story, based on fiction, which I heard secondhand from an old farmer, who doesn't exist. So it must be true or urban legend? Confused yet? Good! Hello! My name is Diedrich Knickerbocker, and I'm your narrator for today's creepy adventure. Our story takes place in 1790, in a sequestered glen, known by the name of SLEEPY HOLLOW. Speaking of creepy looking, check out this guy.

*(enter ICHABOD whistling and reading a book titled: WITCHCRAFT)*

**ICHABOD:** Oh, I do love these ghost stories!

**DIEDRICH:** Hey sir! Watch where you're going. There have been many terrors of the night down that path.

**ICHABOD:** Really?

**DIEDRICH:** Yes! There's a drowsy, dreamy influence that seems to hang over the land.

**ICHABOD:** Sounds fascinating!

**DIEDRICH:** No. Sounds spine-chilling! Why, in the name of all things weird, would you want to go THERE?!

**ICHABOD:** I am a student of supernatural stories and marvellous beliefs!

**DIEDRICH:** Well then, crazy's waiting for you just down the road!

**ICHABOD:** Oh goody! *(walks towards "town" offstage)*

**DIEDRICH:** I tried to warn him.

*(ICHABOD enters, looks around)*

**ICHABOD**: Well, this town looks like a wonderful place to stay for a while.

*(enter WIVES who stop ICHABOD)*

**WIFE 1**: And who might you be?

**ICHABOD**: My name, dear ladies, is Ichabod Crane. *(he bows)*

**WIFE 2**: And what do you do?

**ICHABOD**: I am a schoolmaster.

*(WIVES look at each other happily)*

**WIFE 3**: We are looking for a teacher.

**ICHABOD**: As well as a singing-master. *(starts singing)*

**WIFE 4**: That's fantastic!

**ICHABOD**: But, I'm afraid I don't have much money or a place to stay.

**WIFE 1**: That's ok. If you teach our children, we will gladly house and feed you... a total stranger!

**WIFE 2**: Yes. We don't believe in stranger danger here and you look smart, I think.

**WIFE 3**: That's right! We have a lot stranger things to worry about than random people coming through our town!

**WIFE 4**: Like marvellous tales of ghosts and goblins!

**WIFE 1**: And haunted fields!

**WIFE 2**: And haunted brooks!

**WIFE 3**: And haunted bridges!

**WIFE 4**: And haunted houses!

**ICHABOD**: And the supernatural?!

**WIVES**: Oh, yes!

**ICHABOD**: Then I'm staying! Now, tell me some stories!

*(WIVES start telling a story as they ALL walk offstage; DIEDRICH remains)*

Sneak peek of
# The Hound of the Baskervilles for Kids
### Sir Henry Baskerville

*(enter SHERLOCK, WATSON, opposite MORTIMER, HENRY missing shoe)*

**MORTIMER:** This is Sir Henry Baskerville.

**HENRY:** Hello, Mr. Holmes. I have a little puzzle.

**SHERLOCK:** Yes?

**HENRY:** I received THIS mysterious letter!

*(made from newspaper clippings)*

**WATSON:** *(reading)* As you value your life keep away from the moor. *(hands to SHERLOCK)*

**HENRY:** What do you make of this?

**SHERLOCK:** Well... they used yesterday's Times, as these words are from that newspaper.

**HENRY:** *(observing newspaper)* By thunder, you're right!

**SHERLOCK:** Highly educated people read The Times, yet the envelope address is sloppy.

**MORTIMER:** So?

**SHERLOCK:** So?! Watson, please...

**WATSON:** So... educated with sloppy writing implies intentional deception!

**SHERLOCK:** Exactly!

**MORTIMER:** Now wait a minute, this is the region of guesswork.

**SHERLOCK:** No! We are in the region of probabilities and the scientific use of the imagination.

**MORTIMER:** Very well.

**SHERLOCK:** Furthermore, this was written in a hotel.

**HENRY:** How do you know?

**SHERLOCK:** Elementary, Henry. Look at the writing. The ink has failed many times. Now, if he used his own pen, it would not have failed. I am certain, if we look at hotels near yours for a cut-up Times, we will find our man!

**HENRY:** Excellent!

**SHERLOCK:** Before we go, has anything else of interest happened to you?

**HENRY:** Yes! Someone stole my boot! *(points at foot)*

**SHERLOCK:** Verrrry odd. I happened to notice this detail. It's probably nothing.

**HENRY:** Probably nothing?! It's blatantly added in the middle of this play! It has...

**WATSON:** NO SPOILERS! (motions to audience) Perhaps someone is trying to warn you?

**HENRY:** Or scare me away.

**SHERLOCK:** Let's meet for lunch and we can discuss further.

*(ALL say goodbye; HENRY and MORTIMER exit)*

**SHERLOCK:** Your hat and boots, Watson, quick! Not a moment to lose!

**WATSON:** Shall I run on and stop them?

**SHERLOCK:** Not for the world, my dear Watson. The game's afoot! Someone's following them and we are going to find out who!

**WATSON:** Fun!

*(SHERLOCK and WATSON exit; HENRY and MORTIMER casually walk across and exit; BEARDED MAN enters and follows; as BEARDED MAN nears exiting, enter SHERLOCK and WATSON, behind)*

**SHERLOCK:** There's our man, Watson!

*(BEARDED MAN rushes off stage; SHERLOCK and WATSON follow, then re-enter)*

**SHERLOCK:** He got away in a cab.

**WATSON:** Blimey!

**SHERLOCK:** We are dealing with a very clever man, Watson. Whether good or bad is unknown.

# ABOUT THE AUTHORS

**AMANDA RUBY** earned a BA (Edinboro University) and an MA (Kent State) in theatre. Over the years she has acted, directed, designed costumes, been a dramaturg, and taught theatre to college kids (whether they liked it or not). She created and runs an after-school theatre program at local Elementary and Middle schools called Acting Up! Amanda also enjoys producing plays for her local community theatre. When she isn't at a school or theatre, she really loves being at home with her two kids and husband.

**BRENDAN P. KELSO** came to writing modified Shakespeare scripts when he was taking time off from work to be at home with his newly born son. "It just grew from there". Within months, he was being asked to offer classes in various locations and acting organizations along the Central Coast of California. Originally employed as an engineer, Brendan never thought about writing. However, his unique personality, humor, and love for engaging the kids with The Bard has led him to leave the engineering world and pursue writing as a new adventure in life! He has always believed, "the best way to learn is to have fun!" Brendan makes his home on the Central Coast of California and loves to spend time with his wife and kids.

# CAST AUTOGRAPHS

Printed in Great Britain
by Amazon